Contents

Europe 1914

NORWAY

SWEDEN

RUSSIAN EMPIRE

DENMARK

BRITAIN

NETHERLANDS

GERMANY

BELGIUM

LUXEMBURG

FRANCE

SWITZERLAND

AUSTRO-HUNGARIAN EMPIRE

ROMANIA

BLACK SEA

BOSNIA

SERBIA

BULGARIA

ITALY

TURKEY IN EUROPE

SPAIN

MONTENEGRO

TURKEY

GREECE

MEDITERRANEAN SEA

N

0   500 km

onfle .

DON
£4.50 HIS

NAZI POWER

In Germany

GREG THIE JEAN THIE

Stanley Thornes (Publishers) Ltd

Originally published in 1989 by Hutchinson Education

Reprinted in 1990 by
Stanley Thornes (Publishers) Ltd
Old Station Drive
Leckhampton
CHELTENHAM GL53 0DN
England

Reprinted 1991

British Library Cataloguing in Publication Data

Thie, Greg
 Nazi power in Germany
 I. Title   II. Thie, Jean
 943.085

ISBN 0 7487 0196 6

Designed by Heather Richards

Set in Times and Helvetica by Tek Art Limited

Printed and bound in Great Britain at The Bath Press, Avon

To Michael, James, Tom and Anna-Clare

Acknowledgements

The authors and publisher are grateful to the
following for permission to reproduce text extracts,
photographs and illustrative material used in this
book.

Bundesarchiv 6(1), 9(D), 27, 42, 43, 50, 90, 93; Mary
Evans Picture Library 6(A); The Marquess of Bath
7(E); Christabel Bielenberg, 'The Past is Myself',
(Corgi 1988); Bilderdienst Suddeutscher Verlag 7(5),
34, 57, 71(F), 80; Presseillustration Heinrich R.
Hoffman 6(3), 8(10), 11(20), 46, 90; Hulton Picture
Company 8(C), 24, 32; Ullstein Bilderdienst 10(18),
11(22), 16, 60; Wiener Library 12(O), 51(G),
52(lower), 58, 60, 71(G), 75(E), 76, 77, 79, 85, 91;
Camera Press 9(G), 26, 52(top), 63, 67, 95; Punch
43; David Irving Collection 22, 51(I), 81, 85, 90;
Library of Congress 29; State Institute of War
Documentation, Amsterdam 36, 37; Greg Thie 55;
Rolf Stein Collection 69; Daily Mail 81, 88; National
Film Archive 64, 65; Anne Frank Stichting,
Amsterdam 71, 92, 93, 94.

Picture research by Deborah Manley
Illustrations by Michael Hodson Designs
Map and diagrams by John Booth, Capricorn
Graphics

Hitler and his times

The following pages contain pictures and written evidence covering the years from 1888 to 1945.

These years were chosen for a reason. Adolf Hitler was born in 1889. In the years that followed he built up and led the political party that was known as the Nazi Party. In 1933 he became the leader of Germany and within six years the Second World War had broken out. Germany lost that war and Hitler killed himself as the war ended in 1945.

The top section of each page shows episodes from the life of Hitler. The bottom sections show events happening at the same time in Germany and the rest of the world.

At first, you will not be able to make connections between the two, but as the years pass you should notice that the life of Hitler becomes more and more involved with the lives of the German people and comes to affect the lives of almost everyone on Earth.

As you may already know, historians work with a great variety of sources, as these pages show you. They describe such sources as being either 'primary' or 'secondary'.

Primary sources are those that come from the same time as the event or are contemporary. We usually stretch this definition to include memoirs, autobiographies and interviews, which may be written or given at a later date.

Secondary sources are those that come from accounts written by historians, biographers, TV writers etc, who have examined and weighed up the information in the primary sources.

When you have read these next few pages, you are going, among other things, to look at the sources in these pages as primary and secondary sources and judge their value to a historian.

1 Hitler as a baby.

2 From *Hitler's Letters and Notes* by Werner Masur, 1974.

" ━━━━━━━━━━━━━━━━━━━━━━━━━

Adolf Hitler was born on 20th April, 1889 in Braunau-am-Inn in Austria. His mother loved and spoiled him and so did the rest of the family. After the death of his brother Gustav and sister Ida and of his youngest brother Otto in 1887 he became the apple of both his parents' eyes.

━━━━━━━━━━━━━━━━━━━━━━━━━ "

3 Adolf Hitler at school in 1900.

4 From *Hitler's Table Talk 1941–44.*

" ━━━━━━━━━━━━━━━━━━━━━━━━━

The teachers had no sympathy with young people – their one aim was to stuff our brains and turn us into educated apes – like themselves.

━━━━━━━━━━━━━━━━━━━━━━━━━ "

A Punch cartoon of the leaders of Austria, Germany and Italy.

B From Haydn's *Dictionary of Dates*, 19th edition, 1889.

" ━━━━━━━━━━━━━━━━━━━━━━━━━

Austria signs Defensive Treaty with Germany against Russia, published February 1888. Visit of German Emperor to Vienna, 3rd October, 1888. Fortieth anniversary of Emperor Franz Josef of Austria-Hungary coming to the throne. 2nd December 1888. Suicide of the heir to the Austrian throne, February 1889.

━━━━━━━━━━━━━━━━━━━━━━━━━ "

C From *The War in the Air*, a prophetic novel by H.G. Wells, begun in 1907.

" ━━━━━━━━━━━━━━━━━━━━━━━━━

No-one troubled over the real dangers to mankind. They saw their armies and navies grow larger; they built up their stocks of explosives; they allowed jealousies of other countries to grow.

━━━━━━━━━━━━━━━━━━━━━━━━━ "

5 Hitler at 16, sketched by a friend. ▶

6 Dr Hünes, one of Hitler's teachers, talking in 1923.

" ━━━━━━━━━━━━━━━━━━━━━━━━━━━

Hitler had definite talent ... but he lacked self-discipline – being wilful, arrogant and bad-tempered ... He demanded that his fellow pupils obey him as a leader.

━━━━━━━━━━━━━━━━━━━━━━━━━━━ "

7 Letter from Hitler to a friend, July 1908.

" ━━━━━━━━━━━━━━━━━━━━━━━━━━━

Dear Friend,
To begin with I am still in Vienna and am staying on. Still I am quite enjoying my hermit's life ... I have no other news to tell you except that I caught a gang of bedbugs floating dead in my own blood and that my teeth are chattering.

━━━━━━━━━━━━━━━━━━━━━━━━━━━ "

D From *1910 Census*

" ━━━━━━━━━━━━━━━━━━━━━━━━━━━

The population of Austria-Hungary in 1910:

Germans	12 million	23 %
Magyars	10 million	19%
Rumanians	3 million	6%
Slavs	23.5 million	45 %
Others (eg Italians)	2.5 million	7%

━━━━━━━━━━━━━━━━━━━━━━━━━━━ "

E Parliament building in Vienna; painted by Adolf Hitler.

8 From *Mein Kampf* (My Struggle) by Adolf Hitler (1924) on his reactions to the outbreak of war in 1914.

" For me these hours came as a deliverance from the distress that had been with me during the days of my youth. I am not ashamed to admit that I was carried away by the enthusiasm of the moment. I sank down upon my knees and thanked Heaven for allowing me to be alive at such a time. "

9 From *The First World War* by A.J.P. Taylor, 1963.

" In the early summer of 1916 Hitler's regiment moved south, just in time to take part in the battle of the Somme. It began with an English attack so relentless that almost 20,000 English were killed on the first day alone. "

10 Hitler wearing the Iron Cross.

G From *Hitler* by John Toland, 1976.

" There was a last attack on 13th November. In all the British lost 420,000 – the Germans, 450,000. "

H From the novel *All Quiet on the Western Front* by Erich Maria Remarque, 1929.

" And men will not understand us – for the generation that grew up before us already had a home and a calling and the generation that has grown up after us will be strange to us and push us aside. The war will be forgotten. We will grow older, a few will adapt, some will give in – most will be bewildered. The years will pass by and in the end we shall fall into ruin. "

F Munich crowd welcomes war, 1st August 1914.

11 Comment, in 1931, by Mend, a soldier who fought alongside Hitler in the war.

66

Hitler looked at the rifle with delight which made me secretly laugh.

99

12 An Austrian soldier's comment about Hitler to Mend in 1915.

66

He is just an odd character and lives in his own world, but otherwise he's a nice fellow.

99

13 Fritz Weidmann, Hitler's officer, commenting in 1964.

66

We found out very soon which messengers we could rely on most.

99

14 From a speech by Hitler in 1923.

66

We have the duty to speak, since in the near future, when we have gained power, we shall have the further duty of taking the November criminals and hanging them.

99

15 From a speech by Hitler in Munich, 1923.

66

Do we wish to restore Germany to freedom and power? If 'yes', then the first thing to do is to rescue it from the Jew who is ruining our country. We want to stir up a storm.

99

◄ **I German prisoners of war.**

J From a speech by the President of the German Health Department in 1923.

66

The height to which prices have climbed may be shown by the fact that as of February 15th food prices have risen 500 times in ten years. For many people meat is rare. A million and a half German families lack fuel. Thousands spend their lives in poor primitive houses. Health levels are falling.

99

16 Hitler using his hands while speaking.

17 Comment by Strasser in 1940.

" I have been asked many times what is the secret of Hitler's extraordinary power as a speaker. I think it is intuition. He enters a hall. He sniffs the air. For a minute he gropes, feels his way, senses the atmosphere. Suddenly he bursts forth. His words go like an arrow to their target, he touches each private wound, telling each what he wants to hear. "

18 In relaxed mood.

19 Winston Churchill in 1935 (British Prime Minister, 1940–1945).

" Those who have met Hitler face to face have found a highly competent, cool, well-informed man with an agreeable manner, a disarming smile and few have been unaffected by a subtle personal magnetism. "

K Dr Külz, German minister in 1932.

" The elected Reichstag (parliament) is totally unable to function. The Communists have made gains almost everywhere. If things are faced squarely it seems that more than half the German people have declared themselves against the present state, but have not said what sort of state they would accept. "

L Court report, 1935.

" The German Supreme Court has decided that persons with Jewish blood may not adopt non-Jewish children. Only non-Jew Aryans could bring up an Aryan child in the proper way. "

M Goebbels, Nazi leader, speaking against Communism.

German children greet their leader.

Comment by G. Ward-Price, Daily Mail journalist, writing in 1937.

"

s appearance is healthy, his skin fresh and his pale ue eyes bright. Fondness for children and dogs is a rong trait in Hitler's character.

"

22 Hitler in military uniform.

23 From a speech by Winston Churchill, Britain's Prime Minister, 1941.

"

Hitler is a monster of wickedness, lusting for blood and plunder. Not content with having all Europe under his heel, he must now carry his work of butchery among the vast multitudes of Russia ... this bloodthirsty gutter-snipe must launch his armies upon new fields of death and destruction.

"

Jews being made to scrub pavements as nishment for being Jews.

O Speech by Nazi propaganda minister Goebbels, broadcast by radio, February 1943.

"

The English believe that the German people have given up believing in victory. I say to you – do you believe with us and the Führer in the undoubted total victory of the German people? I ask you – do you want total war, so total and radical that we can hardly imagine it?

"

25 Hitler's Weapons Minister Albert Speer recalling, in 1966, Hitler in 1945.

"

Now he was shrivelling up like an old man. His limbs trembled; he walked stooped with dragging footsteps. Even his voice shook and broke when he got excited. His face was pale and swollen; his uniform, which in the past he had kept very neat was now stained by food he had eaten with a shaking hand.

"

◀ **24** Hitler in 1945 only weeks before his death.

P From the *Daily Mail*, Wednesday, 2nd May, 1945.

"

Hitler dead, German radio tells the World . . . surrender begins on three fronts . . . General Patton's drive reaches Hitler's birthplace . . . Make more Germans see horror camps . . . We must never forget Buchenwald and Belsen. Let those names be Hitler's epitaph. Let them be the token of a pledge that there must be no more Hitlers.

"

Q Bodies in a concentration camp mass ▶ grave.

Questions

Use the evidence on pages 6–12 to answer
these questions.

1 Sources **1, 3** and **10** might all have appeared
in the Hitler family photo album.
  a Are they primary sources or secondary
  sources? Explain your answer carefully.
  b Why do historians try to find photographs
  of the people that they write about?
2 Source **A** is a political cartoon from the
British magazine Punch. It is a primary
source telling us the cartoonist's views on the
people shown.
  a How does Source **A** back up the Treaty of
  1888?
  b What part of the Treaty is not covered by
  the cartoon?
3 Look at what Hitler wrote about his feelings
in 1908 and 1914 in Sources **7** and **8**.
  a What contradiction does there seem to be
  between these two comments on his
  youth?
  b How is it possible for people's memories
  of how they felt at a particular time to
  change?
4 In Source **G** some of the horror of war is
clearly shown. Does the evidence in Source
11 suggest that Hitler was a brave soldier or
a mad fool who loved war? Explain your
answer carefully.

5 The Treaty of Versailles in 1919 (see pages
16–17) set out to punish Germany for
causing the First World War. Using the
evidence in Source **14** can you work out
Hitler's views on the peace treaty?
6 Read carefully the descriptions of Hitler in
Sources **17** and **19**, one was written by the
ex-Nazi Strasser and the other by Churchill,
an Englishman.
  a In what ways do the two back each other
  up?
  b What would an historian need to check to
  be sure about the reliability of what these
  men say?
  c What other types of evidence on Hitler's
  personality would contribute to a balanced
  view?
7 Using an excerpt from Churchill's speech in
1941 (Source **23**), state clearly how this
seems to contradict what he says in Source
19. Can you explain how this change is
possible?
8 Albert Speer wrote Source **25** in a book
published in 1966, 21 years after the death of
Hitler.
  a How might this book be useful to the
  historian?
  b In what ways might the historian not find
  this evidence useful?

The World War 1914-1918

In the late summer of 1914, war broke out between a number of European countries. Britain, Russia, France, Belgium and Serbia faced Germany and Austria-Hungary. Nearly everyone in these countries believed that the war would be over by Christmas 1914.

By 1915 it was clear that they were wrong. The armies of the two sides were forced to shelter in trenches for protection against deadly machine gun fire. Even so, the leaders of the countries felt that they must try to advance. Both sides used their huge armies in great battles where neither side gained much land, but both lost thousands of soldiers.

The governments tried to keep up spirits by telling their people how well their armies were doing and how near victory was. They also pointed out how dangerous the enemy was to frighten their people and convince them that they must continue the war.

The posters here are examples of such propaganda published by both sides in the war. Propaganda usually fixes on one main point or theme and ignores the opposite point of view. Think about what was happening when these posters were produced.

A A British poster urging people to enlist in the armed forces.

B A German poster caricaturing a British officer and the British bulldog. The words say, 'He is guilty . . . When you must still fight and bleed . . . when you must make sacrifices . . . when you must economise on fuel . . . when you must use ration books . . . when you can't return to your peace-time work . . . the enemy is England! Therefore stay united. Stay strong. This way you will guarantee Germany's victory.'

A ▲

B ▼

Questions

1 Fit these statements to the posters.
   a We are not fighting ordinary human beings but fearful monsters.
   b It is not the fault of our government that things are as they are.
2 Where do you think posters like these were displayed for maximum effect?
3 Both sides in the war had officials in charge of their propaganda. Give at least three clear aims they would have had to justify such materials.

German resistance to the War

When the war first broke out, it had been very popular. There had not been a large war in Europe for over 40 years. Young men seemed to think that war would be great fun. They imagined themselves leading cavalry charges and capturing prisoners. Instead, the war turned into a nightmare for the front line soldiers. They were pounded by heavy guns, poisoned by gas or mown down by machine-gun fire.

At home, the women, children and old people began to suffer too. The huge numbers of young men killed and injured meant that many families lost their one wage earner. Food and fuel supplies got harder to get as the result of blockades. The one set up by the British navy had stopped goods getting to Germany throughout the war.

As the war continued, there were demands in many countries for peace. In Germany there were demonstrations against the war by women as early as 1915. Later in the war, demonstrations turned into a refusal to support the war at all.

C **A report by the US Ambassador in Berlin, 1915.**

"

Early in the summer, the first demonstration took place in Berlin. About 500 women collected in front of the Reichstag (parliament) building. They were quickly moved away by the police and none of the German newspapers printed what happened . . . The women talked about high prices for food and said that they wanted their men back from the trenches.

"

D **From *The First World War* by historian A.J.P. Taylor, published in 1963.**

"

At the end of October 1918, the German High Seas Fleet was ordered into action . . . The sailors had not fought a battle for more than two years (since the Battle of Jutland when they had been driven back to port by the British fleet) . . . and had been living quietly with their families in the port of Kiel. On the 29th October, they began to mutiny through the streets of the town. The sailors seized the town and news spread throughout Germany. The German government was convinced that revolution would spread across the country. They decided to end the war before this could happen.

"

E **Cartoon from a German magazine in 1916 about the results of the British naval blockade.**

"

Boy: Mummy, what's cooking there?
Mother: Washing, stupid!
Boy: Does it taste nice?

"

Questions

1 a What actions did women and sailors take in Sources **C** and **D**?
  b What did they hope to gain?
  c How did the German government react?
2 How does Source **E** back up the US Ambassador's report (Source **C**)?
3 Does it matter to the historian that the evidence in Sources **C** and **D** comes from foreign observers? If so, explain why.

The End of the War

As the sailors mutinied the war was still going on. The German army in the west had managed to stop any invasion of German lands, but its three commanders knew that it could not do so for ever.

These three commanders (the German Kaiser (Emperor) Wilhelm II, Field Marshall Paul von Hindenburg and General Ludendorff) decided to send Prince Maximilian, a non-soldier, to ask for a cease-fire from the Allies. In 1917 the United States had come into the war. Prince Maximilian was told by US President Woodrow Wilson that the winning countries would not make deals with the German war leaders. Germany must have a new civilian government.

On his return, Prince Max told the Kaiser that he must give up the throne. When Wilhelm refused, Prince Max simply announced that he *had* abdicated anyway. The Kaiser knew that he was beaten and fled across the border to Holland.

Prince Max then asked the leader of the biggest political party in Germany to become the new German Chancellor. On 9th November 1918, Friedrich Ebert, leader of the SPD (the Social Democratic Party) took over the peace negotiations. A cease-fire was agreed for 11th November 1918.

The treaties to finally end the war took a year to complete. Throughout that time the British kept up their blockade. Food and fuel supplies grew even more scarce. The Germans had to accept the demands of the Allies or face restarting the war.

The treaty that dealt with the future of Germany was called the Treaty of Versailles after the town outside Paris where it was signed.

Similar treaties were signed by other countries that had fought on the German side.

A **The headline from a German newspaper dated 9th November 1918.** The headlines read: 'The Kaiser has abdicated. Abdication of the Crown Prince. Ebert becomes Chancellor. Calling of national assembly.'

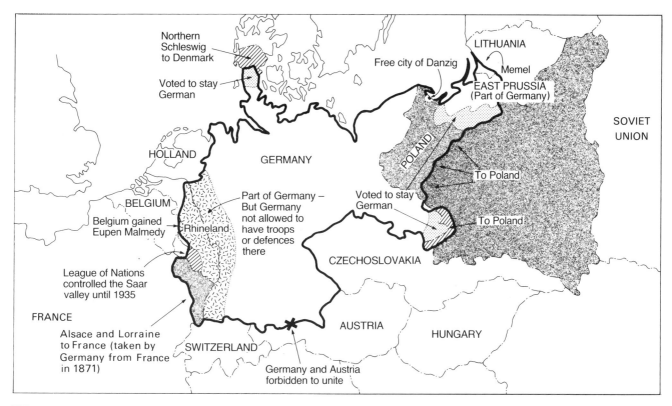

B **Europe and the Treaty of Versailles.**

C **The Treaty of Versailles had 440 parts. Here are just some that the Germans had to agree to or continue the war.**

"

Article 170
Germany is forbidden to buy weapons, ammunition, or any other war material.

Article 191
Building or buying any submarine is forbidden to Germany.

Article 198
Germany's armed forces must not include air forces.

Article 231
Germany accepts responsibility for causing all loss and damage as a consequence of German aggression.

Article 232
Germany must therefore compensate for all damage done to the civilian population of the Allies.

"

Questions

Look carefully at the map (Source **B**) and the major points of the Treaty of Versailles (Source **C**).

1 a Is Source **A** primary or secondary evidence?
  b Do you consider newspapers are always reliable sources of evidence? Explain your answer.
  c What use is *the* newspaper extract (**A**) as evidence?
2 Explain the following two statements. Who do you think made them?
  a Germany must be punished for causing the war.
  b The peace treaty should prevent another world war taking place.
  Do they represent the views of one person or lots of people? In what ways do you see these views demonstrated in the Peace Treaty?

Follow-on Question
3 What problems might be caused by the Treaty of Versailles? You should use all the evidence in this chapter.

The new Republic in trouble

A How the Weimar Constitution was organised.

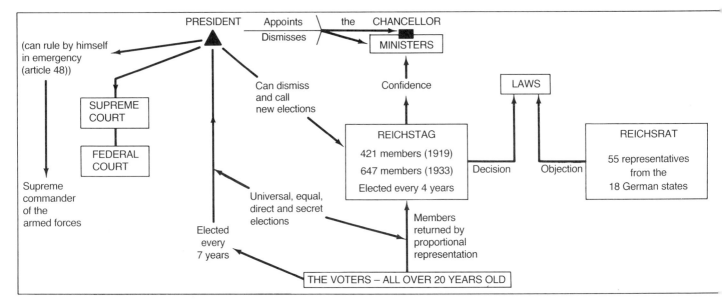

The effects of the Russian Revolution

During the First World War a Communist government had taken over in Russia. This had a number of effects:

a Russia's new rulers decided to stop fighting the Germans and make a peace separate from their allies, Britain, France and the United States of America.

b Germany agreed to end her war with Russia at the Treaty of Brest-Litovsk, but Russia had to give up huge amounts of land and raw materials to Germany.

c Many people in other countries wanted Communism in their country. They believed that Communism would be fairer to the ordinary working person.

The Spartacus Revolt

On the same day as Ebert was taking over as German Chancellor, a group of German Communists (the 'Spartacists'), led by Karl Liebknecht and Rosa Luxemburg, announced that they were setting up a Communist government of workers and soldiers in Berlin. Ebert also had to deal with the sailors' mutiny around Kiel.

At the beginning of 1919, Ebert's government decided to use force. The army was called in. Thirty sailors were shot. The Spartacists were defeated, their leaders shot and their bodies thrown into a canal.

Yet the government had not found it easy to get enough regular troops to put down these revolts. The majority of soldiers just wanted to get home and out of uniform. Volunteers had been recruited to fight and these volunteers now formed themselves into a sort of military force, called the Freikorps.

The Freikorps

Major Kurt von Schleicher set up the Freikorps, and Ebert accepted their help. There were nearly a quarter of a million volunteers, mainly middle class and anti-Communist. They learned how to fight in the streets and the countryside, using armoured cars and other weapons.

The Ebert government (now called the Weimar government after the town to which it had moved in order to escape the violence in Berlin) were to make use of the Freikorps on more than one occasion.

B Results of the first elections to the new National Assembly, 19th January 1919.

	Number of seats	% vote
Social Democratic Party (SPD)	163	37.9
German Democratic Party (DDP)	75	18.6
Central and Bavarian Peoples' Party (Centre/BVP)	91	19.7
German National People's Party (DNVP)	44	10.3
Independent Social Democratic Party (USPD)	22	7.6
German People's Party (DVP)	19	4.4
Other parties	7	1.5
Total number	421	

The Kapp Putsch, 1920

Although Ebert had made use of the Freikorps, he did not have the power to stop them being affected by the Treaty of Versailles. The German armed forces were to be cut right back. Only a small professional army was allowed. Many of the soldiers in the Freikorps feared that they would be unemployed.

When the Berlin Freikorps was ordered to disband, they refused to do so. Instead they marched into the city led by Wolfgang Kapp, a former civil servant. The German government left the city, and Kapp tried to form a new government.

The Reichswehr (German army) did little to stop Kapp. It was the ordinary workers of Berlin who defeated Kapp and the Freikorps. They brought the whole city to a standstill by calling a general strike. Kapp and his supporters gave up, and Kapp left Germany.

Inflation

The Treaty of Versailles had placed all the costs of the war onto the Germans. They were told that they must pay some 150 million marks in reparations (payment for war damage). Although the actual amount to be paid was changed by the Allies several times, Germany claimed that she could not pay.

The value of the German mark fell steadily between 1920 and 1922 as inflation increased. By the end of 1921 the German government announced that it was unable to pay any more reparations.

The French and Belgians did not believe the Germans. As a result, they ordered their troops to occupy the rich industrial area of Germany called the Ruhr in 1923. They intended to take what they needed if the Germans would not pay up voluntarily.

C **Extract from John Toland's 'Adolf Hitler' published in 1976.**

“

On January 11th, 1923, French and Belgian troops marched into the Ruhr on the excuse that Germany had failed to fulfil her promises . . . This quickened the fall in the German mark.

”

D **French soldier guarding German coal taken from the Ruhr.**

Questions

1 Look at Source **A**, the diagram of the Weimar constitution.
   a The German Chancellor was the leader of the party with the most elected members. How did German voters feel they played a democratic part in who became Chancellor? Use the terms secret elections, proportional representation and regular elections to explain your answer.
   b What powers did the President have which made him a powerful person in the Weimar Government?
2 Many of the German political parties had very similar names. If we assume they chose their names to fit their ideas, how do you think the SPD and the DNVP differed?
3 What evidence is there that the Germans put up some resistance to their coal being taken by France?

What inflation did

A Extract from Konrad Heiden's 'Der Führer'.

"

On Friday afternoons in 1923, very long lines of workers waited outside the pay windows of the big German factories, department stores, banks and offices, watching the clock until at last they reached the pay window and received a bag full of paper bank notes.

According to the figures on the notes they were worth anything from seven hundred thousand marks up to 380 billion or even 18 trillion marks. The figures rose month by month, then week to week, then day to day.

People began running as soon as they could. They dashed to the food stores where there were more slow queues. Had you got there first, a half kilo of sugar might have been bought for 2 million marks. If you were at the back, by the time you got to the counter, 2 millions would buy only a quarter kilo.

The government printing presses could not keep up. People carried their money around in sacks or prams. Life was madness, nightmare, desperation, chaos . . .

"

B A woman quoted in 'Wages in Germany', published in 1960.

"

As soon as I received my salary I rushed out to buy what I needed. My daily salary was just enough to buy one loaf of bread and a small piece of cheese . . . A friend of mine, a vicar, came to Berlin to buy some shoes with his month's wages for his baby. By the time he arrived, he only had enough to buy a cup of coffee.

"

C Extract from speech by Health Minister, February 1923.

"

This shocking decline in health conditions applies to the whole of Germany. In the country areas where farmers can feed themselves, conditions seem to be better. But in the towns, . . . there has been a decided decline.

Especially hard hit are the middle class, those living on small sums given annually, the widows and the pensioners who, with their modest incomes, cannot afford today's prices . . . Death rates are rising . . . as are deaths from hunger . . .

"

D A thousand mark note in 1910.

E How the German mark lost its value.

July 1914	£1 = 20 marks
Jan 1919	£1 = 35 marks
Jan 1920	£1 = 256 marks
Jan 1921	£1 = 256 marks
Jan 1922	£1 = 764 marks
Jan 1923	£1 = 71,888 marks
July 1923	£1 = 1,413,648 marks
Sept 1923	£1 = 3,954,408,000 marks
Oct 1923	£1 = 1,010,408,000,000 marks
Nov 1923	£1 = 1,680,800,000,000,000 marks

F One million mark note 1923, printed on one side only.

G A 5 billion mark credit note issued in 1923.

Questions

1 a How many pounds was the German bank note in Source **D** worth in 1914?

 b How many pounds was the note in Source **F** worth in 1923?

2 a Use Sources **A, B** and **C** to explain the statement in Source **A** on page 20 "A half kilo of sugar might have cost 2 million marks."

 b How do Sources **A** and **B** back each other up?

 c Did all German people suffer the same degree of hardship during this time? Use Source **C** to explain your answer in detail.

3 Draw a cartoon to show the practical problems of inflation in Germany in 1923.

Follow-on questions

4 Why did the invasion of the Ruhr cause the value of the German mark to drop even faster?

5 Use the words below to make a web diagram. You need to put the Weimar Government in the centre. Put a box around each of the main problems facing the Weimar Government. Use different colours to link up the following people, events and ideas.

Communism ● high cost of living ●

violence ● Freikorps ● soldiers ●

Treaty of Versailles ● Wolfgang Kapp

WEIMAR GOVERNMENT

Rosa Luxemburg ● reparations

German workers ● France ● Ruhr

Kurt von Schleicher ● inflation ● Spartacists

army revolution

Use the Glossary on pages 92-95 if there are words you are not sure about.

Adolf Hitler 1889-1923

In November 1923, with the inflation at its height, an attempt was made to overthrow the government of Bavaria, one of the largest German states.

About 2000 members of a political party known as the National Socialist German Workers' Party tried to take control of the capital city of Bavaria, Munich. The leader of the National Socialists was 34 year old Adolf Hitler. Most Germans had never heard of him before 1923. What had brought him to this armed rising?

A From Hitler's 'Mein Kampf', 1924

" ────

I did not want to become a civil servant like my father. All of his efforts to inspire me with love or pleasure in his job made me yawn, grow sick to my stomach at the thought of sitting in an office . . . unable to call myself master of my own time.

──── "

B From 'Hitler's Letters and Notes' by Werner Maser, 1974.

" ────

In 1907 Hitler went to Vienna convinced he would easily pass the entrance examinations of the Art Academy . . . he was wrong. In November he returned home to look after his dying mother but returned to Vienna when she died.

──── "

C Hitler's mother.

D From 'Hitler's Letters and Notes'.

" ────

After the deaths of his father and mother Adolf had 100 crowns income each month . . . At that time, a young lawyer earned 70 crowns a month, a primary school teacher 66 crowns and a post office clerk 60 crowns.

──── "

E From Hitler's 'Mein Kampf', 1924.

" ────

As a boy and a young man I had often felt the need to prove by action that my nationalist feelings were not empty.

To me, those hours (of the outbreak of the First World War) seemed like release from the painful feelings of youth . . . A fight for freedom had begun.

──── "

F The arrow points to Hitler.

G From 'Adolf Hitler' by Alan Bullock, 1952.

"

In December 1914 he had been awarded the Iron Cross (2nd class). In August 1918 he was awarded the Iron Cross (1st class) – a medal seldom given to corporals like Hitler or anyone below officer rank.

"

H Hitler in 'Mein Kampf' on the German surrender in 1918.

"

Everything went black before my eyes as I staggered back to my hospital ward and buried my aching head between blankets and pillow . . . the following days were terrible to bear and the nights worse . . . my hatred grew for this terrible crime.

"

I War records of 2nd Bavarian Infantry Regiment

"

During the war, Hitler proved to be a brave and thoughtful comrade who took part in some 50 major and minor military engagements.

"

J From 'Adolf Hitler' by Alan Bullock.

"

After leaving the hospital where he had been treated for the effects of a gas attack, Hitler made his way to Munich. He still drew rations and pay from the army.

"

K Letter sent by Hitler 1921.

"

During the Communist attempt to take over in Munich I remained with the army . . . As an education officer I attacked in my talks the bloodthirsty Red dictatorship . . . In June 1919 I joined the German Workers Party, then with seven members, and in which I believed that I had found a political movement in keeping with my ideals. Today it has grown to 4,5000, and I take personal credit for most of this.

"

L Hitler at 30 years of age.

M Handwriting expert in 1970. The expert was told that the letter was from an unidentified 26 year old soldier.

"

What strikes first is the writer's excitability and restlessness. This shows high aggression . . . also lack of feeling and care of others. War will suit him . . . the writer is highly intelligent but this is shown through cunning and slyness . . . He is able to take in a great deal of information quickly.

"

Hitler becomes Party leader

A Painting entitled 'In the Beginning was the Word'.

The German Workers Party that Hitler first visited in 1919 had only been started a few months before by a Munich locksmith called Drexler. It had about forty members and a committee of six. Hitler listened but also made a speech against one of the members who argued that Bavaria should break with Germany and join with Austria.

This speech impressed the committee and he was invited to become a member.

Uncertain at first whether to go, he eventually turned up at the pub where the meeting was to be held. He discovered that the Party had only a few marks in funds. There was no party programme, no pamphlet, no membership card, not even a party stamp. Nevertheless, he accepted the offer to join the committee as its seventh member.

Hitler now threw himself into the task of organising the Party and building up the membership.

In 1920 he was put in charge of Party propaganda. He organised bigger and bigger meetings. In this he had the support of another party member, Captain Ernst Röhm – a member of the Army Command in Munich. He encouraged ex-soldiers to join to form strong-arm squads for the Party.

In a very short time, Hitler had made a great number of changes to Drexler's small party. The name was changed to the National Socialist German Workers' Party. Hitler drew up and first revealed the Twenty-Five points Source **E**. Although the other committee members were involved in these points it soon became clear to them that Hitler was not interested in many of them, except as a way of getting more support. By 1922, the committee had gone and Hitler was leader of the Party.

B Hitler in 'Mein Kampf', 1924.

"

The manner of getting members rather amazed me, and I did not know whether to be angry or to laugh at it. Hitherto I had not any idea of entering a party already in existence but wanted to found one of my own . . . I should never have entered one of the big parties . . . but this funny little group . . . not yet fossilised into an 'organisation' offered a chance for real opportunity on the part of the individual.

● ● ●

The question of the new flag, kept us very busy in those days (1920). The flag had to be a symbol of our struggle and on the other hand it was necessary that it should have an effect on a large poster . . . After many trials I decided upon a final form – a flag of red material with a white disc bearing in the centre a black swastika . . . and this is how it has remained ever since. At the same time armlets were ordered for the squads who kept order at our meetings. The red expressed the social thought . . . the white the national thought . . . the swastika . . . the struggle for the victory of Aryan mankind.

"

C The flag: the swastika was chosen by Hitler as the symbol for the Nazi Party.

D Extract from a leaflet put out by the Nazi Party committee in 1921.

"

A lust for power and personal ambition have caused Adolf Hitler to return here (from a visit to Berlin) . . . He sees the time as ripe for causing arguments and splitting the party by means of the shadowy people behind him, and thus furthers the interests of the Jews and their friends. It grows more and more clear that his purpose is to simply use the National Socialist Party as a springboard for his own immoral purposes and to

seize the leadership in order to force the Party onto a different track at the psychological moment . . . If any members ask him how he lives and what was his last job, Hitler always becomes angry and excited (and) up to now no answer has been supplied.

"

E Extracts from the 25 Points of National Socialism.

"

We demand the joining together of all Germans on the grounds of self determination.
We demand the right to enough land to support our people.
Only Germans of German blood can be citizens. No Jew can be a citizen.
No further immigration by non-Germans and that those who arrived after 1914 should leave.
We demand the abolition of all unearned income.
We demand support for a healthy middle class.
We demand generous old age pensions.
We demand the abolition of the Treaty of Versailles.
We demand a strong central government.

"

Questions

1 Sort out the events into date order:
   a Hitler drew up the 25 Points.
   b Hitler visited the German Workers' Party in 1919.
   c Hitler put in charge of Party propaganda.
   d In spite of the lack of organisation, Hitler accepted membership of the committee.
   e By 1922 the committee had been disbanded and Hitler was leader.
2 In Source **B** what does Hitler suggest were his motives for joining the Party?
3 Does Source **D** agree or disagree with the evidence in Source **B**? Explain your answer carefully in light of who wrote **B**.

Follow-on questions
4 Using the information in the text and the evidence in Source **E**, write two paragraphs to explain Hitler's short and long term aims for the Nazi Party.
5 Look carefully at Source **A**. Explain how this painting might be used in a book about Hitler written by a person who
   a supported Hitler
   b was opposed to Hitler.

The Italian example

While Hitler was still the little known leader of a small German political party, the man in Source **D** had been made Prime Minister of Italy. His name was Benito Mussolini.

Born into a poor family in 1883, Mussolini had at first been a socialist. He broke with his socialist friends when they decided to oppose Italy's entry into the First World War in 1915 on the side of the Allies.

Mussolini fought in the war and was badly wounded. After the war, Italy went through a period of unrest. Mussolini set up the Fascist Movement in 1919. At first this was made up of fighting squads, but in 1921 the fighters became the Fascist Party.

The Fascists grew so powerful that, when in 1922 Mussolini threatened to march on the Italian capital of Rome, the King of Italy asked Mussolini to become Prime Minister.

A **Extract from 'Hitler's Table Talk', 1941.**

"

Don't suppose that events in Italy had no influence on us. The brownshirt (SA uniform) would probably not have existed without the blackshirt (Fascist uniform).

The March on Rome in 1922 was one of the turning points in history. The mere fact that anything of the sort could be attempted and succeed gave us the push we needed.

"

B **From Hitler's 'Mein Kampf', 1924.**

"

At that time (1922) I admit it openly – I had a deep admiration for the man beyond the Alps, whose huge love for his people made him not bargain with Italy's internal enemies but use all means to wipe them out.

"

C **From 'Adolf Hitler' by John Toland, 1976.**

"

He saw himself copying Mussolini – and his march would be to Berlin.

"

D **Benito Mussolini**

Questions

1 Read Source **A** carefully and explain in your own words why Hitler thought Mussolini's march on Rome was so important.
2 From Source **B**, how do you think Hitler considered that Mussolini dealt with opposition and for what reasons?
3 In what ways might Hitler have planned to copy Mussolini as John Toland suggests in Source **C**.

Build up to the Putsch

A Three of the characters in the events of 1923: von Kahr, General Lossow and Ludendorff.

As the inflation worsened and the occupation of the Ruhr continued, it became clear to the Weimar government in Berlin that it could no longer rely on certain areas of the country to stay under its control.

In 1920, in spite of the unsuccessful Kapp putsch in Berlin, the local army commander in Bavaria had got rid of the SPD leader in Munich. He had then set up a right wing government in Bavaria, led by Gustav von Kahr. No left wingers were included in this government.

From 1920 onwards Bavaria attracted all those who wanted to overthrow the Weimar government in Berlin. The volunteer soldiers of the Freikorps ended up there, as did many of the failed Kapp supporters. They all hoped to destroy the Republic set up in 1918. The Bavarian government made no effort to stop their plotting.

Some wanted independence for Bavaria; others wanted the German Emperor to return; yet others wanted to replace the Weimar rulers with themselves.

Hitler supported the third view. He set out to convince the Bavarian government that this should be done.

B Extracts from Hitler's speeches, April 1923.

"
Until the present day the half-hearted and lukewarm have remained the curse of Germany . . . For freedom something more is needed than an economic policy; if a people is to become free it needs pride, willpower, defiance, hate, hate and once again hate.

. . . You must say farewell to the hope for action from the Right.
"

By October 1923, the three main figures in the Bavarian government were von Kahr, the leader of the Bavarian government, von Lossow and von Seisser, Chief of the Bavarian State Police. They were united in their dislike of the Weimar government, especially as under its new Chancellor Gustav Stresemann, it had called off resistance to the French in the Ruhr and had agreed to re-start reparation payments.

However, they were all agreed that Hitler's revolutionary ideas were unacceptable. Hitler, on the other hand, suspected that von Kahr and the others were planning to take Bavaria out of Germany altogether. At this point, von Kahr announced that there would be a big public meeting in the Bürgerbraukeller on the evening of 8th November.

Germany and Bavaria.

C **Report to the US government, December 1922.**

"
My own forecast on the general attitude of the Bavarians is that sooner or later a serious break is going to come from here. Hitler is . . . working very slowly . . . along the same lines as Mussolini. He is getting a great deal of money from manufacturers as Mussolini did.
"

D **Comment by Helene Hanfstaengl, a confidante of Hitler.**

"
Absolutely no-one could ever persuade him to change his mind, once it was made up. On a number of occasions when his followers tried to persuade him to change I noticed the faraway, unheeding expression in his eyes; it was as though he had closed his mind to all ideas but his own.
"

E **Extracts from Hitler's speeches, 1923.**

"
. . . We must compromise these people so that they have to march with us.

• • •

. . . The German problem will be solved for me only once the black, white and red swastika banner floats over Berlin . . . the hour has come.
"

F **Extract from 'I Know these Dictators' by G. Ward-Price, 1937.**

"
Hitler's plan was simple. Von Kahr and von Lossow and the other important people in Munich would be at the meeting. He decided to seize the occasion to force them to join with him in a rising against the Berlin government.

Several hundred Storm Troopers were secretly armed and with these Hitler surrounded the hall. Three thousand Bavarians sat in the hall listening to von Kahr. Suddenly at 8.45, brown shirted Storm Troopers armed with pistols and a machine gun, pushed into the hall. Hitler fired his revolver at the ceiling, then he shouted, 'The National revolution has begun. The hall is surrounded. No-one must leave. If there is any disturbance I will put the machine gun in the gallery. The army and police have come over to our side. The Bavarian Government is overthrown. The National Government is overthrown. A Provisional Government will be formed. The army and police barracks have been occupied!'

Von Kahr, von Lossow and von Seisser obeyed at once when he ordered them to leave the hall with him. Lossow whispered to the others 'Play for time'.

In a private room Hitler's first words were, 'No-one leaves this room without my orders.' Then he waved his gun and said, 'There are five bullets in my pistol – four for traitors and one, if things go wrong, for myself.' Upon this he named himself Head of the National Government; von Lossow to be Defence Minister; von Seisser, Police Minister; von Kahr, ruler of Bavaria.

Hitler returned to the hall and announced that he was taking control of the National Government. He was loudly cheered. At that moment General Ludendorff appeared, to be offered Supreme Command of the German army. The general declared that 'his honour left him no choice but to accept.'
"

Hitler now received a message that the army engineers were not accepting the Storm Troopers' arguments. Hitler decided to leave the hall and placed General Ludendorff in charge. As soon as Hitler was out of sight, von Lossow said he had to leave if he were to give orders. Ludendorff agreed and let him go, along with von Seisser and von Kahr. When Hitler returned he found all three had disappeared! When Hitler criticised Ludendorff, the latter said that there was no problem. Each of the three had sworn publicly to support what was going on.

G Nazi attempt to win support, the morning of 9th November, 1923.

H Proclamation to the German people announcing the overthrow of the 'Government of the November Criminals' and the setting up of a 'new German Government and its members'.

Proklamation
an das deutsche Volk!
Die Regierung der November-verbrecher in Berlin ist heute für
abgesetzt erklärt worden.
Eine
provisorische deutsche Nationalregierung
ist gebildet worden, diese besteht aus
Gen. Ludendorff
Ad. Hitler, Gen. v. Lossow
Obst. v. Seisser

On the contrary, von Lossow was already ringing loyal army units and making arrangements for them to come to Munich. At 5 am Hitler found out that von Lossow had put out a message denouncing the putsch. Snow was falling as Hitler called back all supporters not holding important positions.

Hitler vetoed a plan to withdraw and fight in the countryside. Instead he decided that they should march through the city. At noon, with Hitler and Ludendorff in the front row, the two thousand marchers set off.

Failure

A From Alan Bullock's 'Hitler: A study in Tyranny', 1952.

"

The column swung down the narrow streets singing as it went. Beyond lay the old War Ministry, where Ernst Röhm, leader of the SA Storm Troopers, was surrounded with his troops. The police waited at the end of the street, guns ready . . . Who fired first has never been settled. Hitler cried out 'Surrender!' At this moment a shot rang out and bullets swept the street. The first man to fall was Scheubner-Richter, with whom Hitler had linked arms. Hitler fell, either pulled down or seeking cover. Goering was badly wounded and carried into a house. All was confusion . . . One man kept his head. Erect and unhurried. Ludendorff marched steadily on through the line of police . . .

"

B From G. Ward-Price's 'I know these Dictators'.

"

Von Scheubner-Richter was amongst those killed. He pulled Hitler down with him as he fell, dislocating his shoulder. Ludendorff stalked stiffly on through the firing police.

"

C From John Toland's 'Adolf Hitler', 1976.

"

Most accounts picture Ludendorff as courageous for staying on his feet and Hitler as cowardly for dropping to the street even though Hitler's arm dislocation indicates that he was dragged down. Robert Murphy testified that, 'both Ludendorff and Hitler behaved in a similar manner, like the battle hardened soldiers they were. Both fell flat to escape the (one minute) hail of bullets'. Another eyewitness, a watchman, also saw Ludendorff throw himself to the ground and then find cover 'behind a corpse or a wounded man'. A second watchman agreed that no-one was standing after the volley (of shots).

"

D Comment by a Nazi official from John Toland's 'Adolf Hitler', 1976.

"

Faced with an oncoming mob, the leader of the State Police ordered his men forwards. All at once he heard a shot zing past his head. It killed a sergeant. Then before I could give an order, my people opened fire. . .

The marchers returned the fire. One of the first was Scheubner-Richter. Another was Graf, who had leapt in front of Hitler to take the half dozen shots meant for him. In falling, the personal body guard clutched Hitler, yanking him down so sharply that his left arm was dislocated. On the other side Scheubner-Richter also helped Hitler to the pavement . . . General Ludendorff (marched) directly, left hand in coat pocket, into the line of fire.

"

Assignment: The Beer Hall Putsch 1923

Using the questions on this page and looking back through the chapters you have read so far, you are going to try to assess the role of an individual in the events of history.

The individual is, of course, Adolf Hitler. You will be looking at his role in the Beer Hall Putsch by examining his character, attitudes and motives at that time. Do you think that the putsch would have taken place without him?

When you are considering this question, try to avoid hindsight – that is being wise after the event! Remember that *none* of the people involved knew what would happen next.

The chapters you will need to look back through are on pages 26–30. The glossary on pages 92–95 will also help you.

Your overall purpose will be to explain briefly the events that led up to the start of the Munich Putsch of 1923. The questions provide a framework to your study.

Questions

1 Give an account of Hitler's life up to the start of the putsch. To do this you should:
   a Identify what you think were the key points of his life (for example, World War I) from 1889 to 1923.
   b List what you think were the main features of his personality, outlook and values.

2 Explain how and why von Lossow, von Seisser and von Kahr became involved in the events of 1923. What do you think they wanted? What part did they play in the events leading up to the putsch?

3 Use the evidence in these chapters, plus any other evidence you may find elsewhere, (for example, the chapter 'The Italian Example') to support this statement:
   'Hitler was the driving force behind the 1923 Putsch and without his influence it would not have taken place.'

4 Collect evidence in the same way to support this statement:
   'The leaders of Bavaria were in the right frame of mind to mount a challenge through revolt in 1923 to the Weimar government. Such a revolt would have happened anyway and did not need Hitler.'

5 Having answered questions 3 and 4, which of your investigations do you think is nearer to the truth of what actually happened? Present your evidence carefully.

6 Look at the sources dealing with the failure of the putsch (page 30). In which ways are the accounts:
   a similar?
   b different?
   c If you do discover differences, how do you explain them?
   d If sources do not agree, does that make all of them useless to the historian? Explain your answer carefully.

7 Many historians consider that the outcome of the putsch marked a turning point in Hitler's approach to achieving power. While you are reading the next chapters that deal with Hitler's rise to power from 1924 to 1933, collect evidence that supports this point of view.

Prison and the Book

Although Hitler was hidden for a few days, he was eventually arrested and put on trial in Munich. The chief witnesses for the prosecution against Hitler were Kahr, Lossow and Seisser!

Once the trial began on 26th February 1924, it was clear that Hitler intended to use it to his own advantage. He took full responsibility for the whole putsch and laid the blame on Seisser, Kahr and Lossow for its final failure. In speech after speech from the dock throughout the twenty-four days of the trial Hitler was allowed to make political points. The judges did little to stop him, except to rebuke members of the public who stood up to applaud Hitler's words.

The results of the trial were that Ludendorff was let off, and Hitler was given the minimum sentence of five years. Even so some of the judges protested that it was too long a sentence. The President of the court calmed them by saying that Hitler would almost certainly be released on probation long before five years had passed.

Hitler was sent back to Landsberg Prison. He had been there since his arrest on 11th November 1923 and he was released on 20th December, 1924. He used the time to write his book – 'Mein Kampf' (My Struggle) – dictated to his secretary Rudolf Hess.

B **Hitler in prison in 1923 with Rudolf Hess, who was to become deputy leader of the Nazi Party (second from the right).**

A **Hitler's dedication of 'Mein Kampf'.**

On November 9, 1923, at twelve-thirty in the afternoon, in front of the Feldherrnhalle as well as in the courtyard of the former War Ministry, the following men fell, with loyal faith in the resurrection of their people:

> ALFARTH, FELIX, *businessman, b. July 5, 1901*
> BAURIEDL, ANDREAS, *hatter, b. May 4, 1879*
> CASELLA, THEODOR, *bank clerk, b. August 8, 1900*
> EHRLICH, WILHELM, *bank clerk, b. August 19, 1894*
> FAUST, MARTIN, *bank clerk, b. January 27, 1901*
> HECHENBERGER, ANTON, *locksmith, b. September 28, 1902*
> KÖRNER, OSKAR, *businessman, b. January 4, 1875*
> KUHN, KARL, *headwaiter, b. July 26, 1897*
> LAFORCE, KARL, *student of engineering, b. October 28, 1904*
> NEUBAUER, KURT, *valet, b. March 27, 1899*
> PAPE, CLAUS VON, *businessman, b. August 16, 1904*
> PFORDTEN, THEODOR VON DER, *County Court Councillor, b. May 14, 1873*
> RICKMERS, JOHANN, *retired Cavalry Captain, b. May 7, 1881*
> SCHEUBNER-RICHTER, MAX ERWIN VON, *Doctor of Engineering, b. January 9, 1884*
> STRANSKY, LORENZ, RITTER VON, *engineer, b. March 14, 1889*
> WOLF, WILHELM, *businessman, b. October 19, 1898*

So-called national authorities denied these dead heroes a common grave.

Therefore I dedicate to them, for common memory, the first volume of this work. As its blood witnesses, may they shine forever, a glowing example to the followers of our movement.

ADOLF HITLER

Landsberg am Lech
Fortress Prison
October 16, 1924

C Hitler's ideas on race: the Aryan from 'Mein Kampf'.

> All that we admire in the world today, its science and its art, its technical developments and discoveries ... is almost completely the product of the Aryan (race) creative power ... therefore he represents the idea of what we understand by the term: MAN. ... for the setting up of superior (Aryan) types of civilisation, it is essential that there should be a supply of inferior races. It is certain that the first stages of human civilisation used inferior races as slaves.

D Hitler compares Aryans to Jews.

> The Jew offers the most striking contrast to the Aryan ... Since the Jew ... never had a civilisation of his own, he has always got what he needed from others ... We must realise that there has never been any Jewish art and that the Jew has produced nothing in either architecture and music that is original ... The Jew lies in wait for the (Aryan) girl, hoping to seduce her and mix up racially pure people ... but as long as a people remain racially pure they can never be overcome by the Jew.

E Hitler on Communist Russia.

> We must not forget the present rulers of Russia are blood stained criminals. It must not be forgotten that the international Jew, who is today the absolute master of Russia, does not look on Germany as an ally but as a country condemned to the same fate as Russia (Communism).

F Hitler on future friends.

> France is and will remain our complete enemy ... England is not pleased to see France too powerful. Great Britain, Italy and Germany should be able to work together.

G Hitler on the majority and the man.

> One thing we must remember and may never forget: a majority can never be the substitute for THE MAN. It always puts forward stupid and cowardly policies; and just as one hundred fools do not make one wise man, an heroic decision is not likely to come from a hundred cowards.

H Hitler on living space.

> In general terms land in Europe is only to be got at the expense of Russia ... Thus Germany must do as it has done before in order to guarantee its daily bread – occupy Russia.

Questions

1 a Why do you think Hitler chose the title 'My Struggle' for his book?
   b Why do you think he dedicated the book to the men listed in Source A?
2 Look at Source B. Does it provide you with any evidence about how Hitler was treated in prison?
3 Read Sources C to H carefully. They are all taken from Hitler's book.
   Write down those things that Hitler says should be done if he and his party come to power. Later, you should be able to compare what is in the book with what Hitler actually did.

Follow-on question
4 Still using the sources C to H consider these questions.
   a Which of Hitler's ideas do you think were most likely to lead to war?
   b Which countries do you think Hitler thought might be involved in such a war and on which side?

Recovery and Collapse: 1924-1930

The inflation that had encouraged the Nazis to make their grab for power in Munich was finally brought under control in 1924. As you read this chapter think about the effect of these events on the German people. What might it have made them think?

The work of bringing inflation under control had been started by the new Chancellor, Gustav Stresemann, who had taken over in 1923 (when Ebert became President). He had called off the policy of non-cooperation with the French that the German workers had been following since the occupation of the Ruhr. His government had also set up a new bank. It had issued a new currency called the Rentenmark. A fixed number of these marks were to be exchanged for the old inflation money that people still had. Reparations were to be paid again to the Allies, so the French and Belgian troops pulled out of the Ruhr.

This whole arrangement was backed by the United States under the Dawes Plan of 1924. The US agreed to lend Germany nearly 800 million dollars.

The results of Stresemann's new policy were soon seen. Business began to revive, wages increased and general working conditions improved. Inflation came under control. Germany began to look prosperous again, but Stresemann knew that everything depended on the US loan.

In 1929 (the year in which Stresemann died of a heart attack) the US experienced the 'Wall Street Crash' (the collapse of the stock market with thousands of people made bankrupt overnight).

This so damaged the American economy that the loans to Germany were called in. In the world depression which followed Germany was hit worst. By 1932 six million Germans were out of work.

C From a speech by Gustav Stresemann in 1928.

66 ━━━━━━━━━━━━━━━━━━━━━━━━━

Germany is dancing on a volcano. If the short term credits (loans) are called in (by the Americans) a large selection of our economy would collapse.

━━━━━━━━━━━━━━━━━━━━━━━ 99

A Painting of night club life in Berlin in the 'golden 1920s' when Berlin was one of the world's favourite cities and perhaps the most culturally productive.

B The Café Krantzler In Berlin in the 1920s.

D Christabel Bielenberg and her gardener talk in 1939. She recalled this in her book 'The Past is Myself', 1968.

" ━━━━━━━━━━━━━━━

Herr Neisse was the son of a Saxon peasant. He had fought in the Great War and returned to the chaos of Berlin a little surprised at the sudden complete German defeat. 'You see we were told of great victories, we seemed to be doing all right and then suddenly finish, the government sued for peace. I came back to Berlin to my Hilde.'

She must have been a great girl because she waited ten years before Herr Neisse collected enough funds to marry her. He tried everything to get a job as a gardener, walking from house to house. He did not drink, or smoke, worked for his lunch and starved for the rest of the day . . . but both he and Hilde managed to save.

Mr Neisse had not known quite who had been to blame for Germany losing the war, but there was no doubt in his mind that what happened in 1923 was the result of a terrible plot.

In the disastrous months of 1923 his savings, Hilde's savings, their hopes all vanished overnight. 'The inflation, you see . . . suddenly we had nothing. With my savings I was able to buy one cup and one saucer. Funny, wasn't it?'

Not funny really, because his voice shook as he spoke . . . The loss of his little bank account shattered whatever faith he had in the Weimar Republic and his own self respect.

Unemployment had followed as many of the middle class people in the town had also been ruined. When their houses were taken over by Jews and shopkeepers, he eventually went to work for them. Slowly, with the aid of Hilde he watched his little allotment grow and for two years they had enough to live on. Aged nearly 40 they at last married . . .

Then came 1929 and a huge wave rolled over Europe and America, leaving a trail of bankruptcies and suicides behind. The Neisses lost the chance to own half a vegetable stall and he lost his job.

He joined an army of 6 million unemployed and, although they did not actually starve because of the allotment, they were back to where they started . . .

Communism did not appeal to him; he had always worked for the better off and didn't want to bust the whole thing up, he just wanted to belong somewhere. National Socialism was more like it. He began to go to Party meetings . . . he was told that the Jews were the evil root of all Germany's ills.

'Oh no, you must not get me wrong, not one particular Jew . . . No, no. International Jewry.'

A party member by 1931, he was given a job by the Nazis. Although he knew of the corruption of party members, he believed Hitler knew nothing of it. 'He is a child lover; he loves dogs too.'

━━━━━━━━━━━━━━━ "

Questions

1 How do sources **A** and **B** indicate that the German economy improved from 1924–29?
2 Do you consider it likely or unlikely that all German people were able to spend time in expensive night clubs as shown in Source **A**? Explain your answer carefully.
3 How accurate was Stresemann's forecast in 1928 (Source **C**)? Give supporting evidence.
4 Christabel Bielenberg was an Englishwoman who married an anti-Nazi German lawyer before the Second World War. Her husband was later arrested for knowing about the July plot to kill Hitler (you will read about this later).

   Read Source **D** carefully and then answer the questions. Use as much evidence from the source as you can to back up your own ideas.
   a What attitude did Herr Neisse have to events at the end of the First World War?
   b What were his views on the events of 1923?
   c What happened to him personally in that year?
   d What attitudes did he have towards Communists?
   e What attitudes did he have towards Jews?
   f Explain why he joined the Nazi Party in 1931.
   g In what way did he see Hitler as different from some of the other Nazis?

A German Democratic Party poster 1924.

" —————————————————————

Translation: Against a new inflation; for German unity and the Republic. Away with our enemies. The DDP brings recovery. Vote German Democratic.

—————————————————————— "

B German National Party poster 1924.

" —————————————————————

Translation: Free from Versailles. Away with the Jewish-Socialist Front. For Freedom and Fatherland. Your solution: German National.

—————————————————————— "

C Bavaria People's Party poster 1928.

" —————————————————————

Translation: As it was 1918; as it is 1928. Therefore vote Bavarian People's Party.

—————————————————————— "

D German Communist Party (KPD) poster 1932.

" —————————————————————

Translation: Away with this system.

—————————————————————— "

E Social Democrat poster 1932.

" —————————————————————

Translation: The worker in the Germany of the swastika! Therefore vote List 1 Social Democrat.

—————————————————————— "

F Nazi Party poster 1932 election.

" —————————————————————

Our last hope . . . Hitler.

—————————————————————— "

C ▲

E ▲

▼ D

▼ F

Hitler comes to power

After the failure of the Munich Putsch, Hitler had taken the decision that the Party must try to take power in as legal a manner as possible. Progress at first was slow.

A Results of the 1928 elections to the Reichstag.

Party	Votes	Seats won
Nazis	810,000	12
Social Democrats	9,153,000	153
Centre/Bavarian		
People's Party	4,658,000	78
Communists	3,265,000	54

By 1930 all that had changed. The elections of that year saw the Nazi vote leap to 6.3 million giving them 107 seats in Parliament. They were now the second largest party in the Reichstag.

In the two years that followed, Nazi support reached its peak. In the July 1932 elections, they increased their vote to 13.7 million (37.4 per cent of the total vote) and had 230 Reichstag seats. They were now the largest party in Parliament.

Earlier in 1932, President Hindenburg (who had taken over after President Ebert's death in 1925) had dismissed the coalition under Brüning which appeared to be making things worse by cutting government spending. Meanwhile the private armies of the Nazis and Communists continued to do battle with each other on the streets.

In an attempt to bring this disorder to an end, Hindenburg gave his support to Franz von Papen. Von Papen could not get support from enough people in the Reichstag, so Hindenburg helped him by ruling by decree (see diagram page 18 showing the President's powers under Article 48 of the constitution).

Von Papen tried to deal with the Nazis. He told Hitler that he intended to call another election at once. After the election Hitler would be asked to join von Papen's government. Hitler refused unless *he* were to head the new government.

Von Papen rejected this and called the election for November anyway. He hoped that the Nazis would lose votes, and in this he was correct. The Nazi vote fell back to 11 million (33.1%) and their share of seats fell to 196 . The Nationalists did well, but the most surprising increase was scored by the Communists, who won 100 seats.

The Communist success alarmed the people in charge of Germany. Hindenburg dismissed von Papen and put in his place a representative of the army, General von Schleicher.

Von Papen continued to scheme his way back to power. He told Hindenburg that the only way to move forward and stop the Communist revival was to make Hitler Chancellor of a coalition government. He, von Papen, would be in the government as Vice-Chancellor where his job would be to control Hitler and the other couple of Nazis allowed into the government.

These guarantees convinced Hindenburg. On 30th January 1933, Hitler was appointed Chancellor of Germany.

B Von Papen after his 1933 appointment

" I have Hindenburg's confidence. Within two months we will have pushed Hitler so far into a corner that he'll squeak. "

C Nazi businessman commenting in 1972.

" Well, really it was the only party that promised to get us out of the hole. Their idea was that this would only be possible if we as a nation developed a team spirit, solidarity and pulling on the same rope instead of quarrelling about petty differences and opinions. "

D Law student commenting in 1972 on his experience of the 1930s.

" What did he promise? Work and bread for the masses, for the millions of workers that were unemployed and hungry at that time. Nowadays work and bread doesn't mean very much but at that time it was an absolute necessity – a basic need . . . and this promise that wouldn't make any sense today – *then* it sounded like a promise of paradise. "

E Printer's son commenting in 1972 on his experience of the 1930s.

> Anyone who said that I will lead you to the promised land, I will deliver you from evil – anyone who said that then would be greeted with enthusiasm. Of course there were those who said 'This is a false prophet'. But who was to know if they were right at that time? No one did.

F A one man political demonstration in 1930. The posters read 'I have been ruined by ► the government'.

G In 1972 an SPD member looks back at this time.

> For the first few minutes he wasn't a good speaker, but then he turned into a terribly good speaker. The whole feeling in the hall became more and more hysterical. He was interrupted after nearly every phrase by great applause and women began screaming. It was like a mass religious ceremony and I kept feeling on and off for a few seconds at a time – 'What a pity I can't share that belief of all those people . . . that I am alone . . . that I oppose all that.' I thought he is talking nonsense, all the old nonsense that I know he always talks . . . But I still felt that it must be wonderful just to jump into that bubbling pot and be a member of all those believers.

Questions

1 a Draw a bar chart to show the number of seats gained by the Nazis in the elections of 1928; 1930; July 1932; November 1932.
   b What do these figures tell you?
   c Give reasons to explain them.
2 What part was played by the following people in the events of 1932–1933.
   a President Hindenburg
   b Franz von Papen
   c General von Schleicher
3 Read sources **C**, **D** and **E**.
   a What did the Nazis promise the German voter?
   b What *two* promises do you think would have had the most appeal to German voters in the 1930s?
4 Using Source **F,** explain why such a man might not have supported the Weimar Government.
5 Why do you think the writer of Source **G** felt sorry that he could *not* join in with the rest of the audience?
6 What techniques were being used by Hitler to gain support for the Nazis?

Totalitarianism

Under a totalitarian regime:
Individuals are thought to be less important than the state or government's ideas about what is good for the whole people. The government tries to get as much control over individuals as possible.

Although totalitarian governments differ throughout the world, you should find most of the features shown below in a totalitarian country.

Democracy

Under a democratic system of government:
Individuals have rights and the government does not expect to have complete control over the people.

Although democracies are very different throughout the world, you should find most of the features shown below in a democratic country.

VOTING SECRET SO VOTERS ARE NOT AFRAID TO VOTE AGAINST THE GOVERNMENT

VOTING BOX

PEOPLE ARE NOT USUALLY PUNISHED FOR SPEAKING AGAINST THE GOVERNMENT: ALTHOUGH THE GOVERNMENT MAY NOT LIKE IT!

THROW THEM OUT!

REGULAR, FREE ELECTIONS IN WHICH VOTERS CAN CHOOSE FROM DIFFERENT PARTIES WHO COMPETE FOR POWER

VOTE FOR ME!

VOTE

CHOOSE ONE OF US TO VOTE FOR!

LAWS ARE MADE BY THE COURTS AND BY THE ELECTED POLITICIANS

CLUBS, SOCIETIES, MEETINGS, LEISURE ACTIVITIES, TRADE UNIONS ETC., ARE NOT USUALLY CONTROLLED BY THE GOVERNMENT

SOME POSSIBILITY THAT CHANGES CAN BE BROUGHT ABOUT EVEN IF THE GOVERNMENT DOESN'T AGREE WITH THEM

PEOPLE CAN GENERALLY READ AND SEE WHAT THEY LIKE, THERE IS LITTLE OR NO CENSORSHIP

THIS GOVERNMENT IS RUBBISH!

THIS GOVERNMENT IS WONDERFUL!

Hitler seizes control

Although Hitler was now Chancellor, he and his supporters were some distance from having complete control of the country. In this chapter you will be seeing how Hitler took complete control.

There were only two other Nazis in the cabinet apart from Hitler: Goering and Frick. Nevertheless, these two worked at once to increase Nazi influence: Goering through the giant Prussian police force that he now headed, and Frick by getting rid of non-Nazi civil servants.

Hitler now aimed to get a clear majority in the Reichstag so that he could get his laws 'rubber stamped' by his own people. He also aimed to keep the support of President Hindenburg (now 86 and President since 1925). Hitler knew that the President kept the right to remove him under the Weimar constitution.

The Nazis decided to call new elections for 5th March 1933.

The time line that follows shows the main events leading up to these elections and the important events that followed. By the end of this period, Hitler and the Nazis had Germany firmly in their grip.

B Hindenburg (left) with Hitler.

A Timeline 1933–1934.

1 Feb 1933	Hitler announced a new autobahn (motorway) construction programme led by Fritz Todt.
2 Feb	Goering set up an auxiliary police force made up of 25,000 SA men and 15,000 SS men.
27 Feb	The Reichstag building burned down.
5 Mar	General election gave the Nazis, with the help of the Nationalists, the majority in Parliament that Hitler wanted.
23 Mar	Law passed by the Reichstag 'for Removing the Distress of People and Reich' known as the Enabling Law. It gave Hitler the right to make his own laws.
31 Mar	Individual state parliaments forced to hold new elections.
7 Apr	New state governors appointed by Hitler.
1 May	May Day declared an official national holiday.
2 May	All trade union offices occupied by SA/SS. Union officials arrested and some sent to concentration camps. All workers and employers were now forced into one union called the German Labour Front led by Robert Ley, and under total Nazi control.
10 May	Books by authors who were Jewish or known to be anti-Nazi publicly burned in Berlin.
10 May	SPD headquarters attacked.
26 May	Communist Party broken up.
22 Jun ↓ 5 July	SPD banned. Bavarian Peoples, National and Centre Parties disbanded
14 July ↓ 20 Sep	All political parties banned except the Nazis. Laws passed to protect farmers' inheritance.
22 Sep	Censorship controlled by Propaganda Ministry.
1934 30 Jan 30 Jun 2 Aug	State parliaments abolished. Night of the Long Knives (see page 44–45) Death of Hindenburg. Hitler becomes Führer (leader) and Reichschancellor.

C Christabel Bielenberg in 'The Past is Myself', 1968.

"

I took note that Hitler had only two other Nazis with him in the cabinet, and that he was well hemmed in by respectable figures like von Papen . . . (but) . . . events moved fast. The burning of the Reichstag, the last free elections, the Enabling Laws, the banning of the Trades Unions and other parties – the whole process of 'Co-ordination' was over and done with by July of that year (1933) . . . it took Hitler exactly six months to manoeuvre himself and his party to power.

"

D Nazis round up political opponents.

E The Enabling Law of 23rd March 1933 signed by Hitler and Frick.

"

Article 1: The National Socialist Workers' is the only political party in Germany. Article 2: Whoever tries to run or form another political party will be punished with prison up to three years – if not a greater penalty.

"

F Sefton Delmer, an English journalist, reports on Hitler and Goering's reaction to the Reichstag fire in February 1933.

"

'This is the beginning of a Communist uprising. Not a moment must be lost,' shouted Goering. He was cut off by Hitler 'Now we'll show them! Anyone who stands in our way will be mown down . . . Every Communist official must be shot . . . all friends of the Communists must be locked up. . .' He shouted that he needed no more proof that the Communists, by 'shamefully setting fire (to the Reichstag), had wished to give the signal for their mass action.'

"

Questions

1 Christabel Bielenberg was an Englishwoman married to a German. In her account of the major events of 1933, she picks out certain things that happened and leaves out others. Explain why you think that she chose those particular events to mention.

2 How do you think her account of that year might differ from those of
a a Communist?
b a Nazi supporter?

3 In what way do Sources **D** and **E** support Christabel Bielenberg's evidence?

4 Look at 'Totalitarianism/Democracy' (pages 40–41). Using the information in that chapter, note down in which ways you think that Hitler and the Nazis had set up a totalitarian state in Germany by the end of 1934.

5 a Look carefully at Source **E**. Can you suggest two completely different reactions to the 14th July law on political parties.
b Explain why the reactions would be so different.

6 Read Source **F** and the section on the Reichstag fire in the glossary.
a Does the evidence indicate that the Nazis set fire to the Reichstag?
b How did Hitler make use of the fire to strengthen his own position?

The Night of the Long Knives

By the beginning of 1934, there were clear differences amongst the Nazi leaders about the way forward. The main difference centred around the role of the SA (Storm Troopers or brown shirts) who formed Hitler's private army.

The SA had been set up in the early days of the Nazi Party. As the 1920s passed, the SA had grown. It had been used not only to protect the Nazi leaders, but to frighten opponents by deliberately smashing up their meetings, starting riots, beating and even murdering people.

These 'old fighters', under their leader Ernst Röhm, expected rich rewards when Hitler became Chancellor in 1933. Instead, many of them now felt cheated. They were disgusted by all the new Nazis who had joined the party since 1933. It seemed that other people were getting the luxuries that *they* should be having.

Röhm tried to convince Hitler that the SA should replace the tiny regular army (the Reichswehr) of 100,000 men. Röhm believed that the way to make sure that the revolution continued was to replace powerful, rich people by the ordinary people who had supported Hitler from the start.

A Röhm quoted in 'Hitler Speaks', published 1933.

> The new army must be revolutionary. You only get the chance once to . . . lift the world off its hinges. But Hitler puts me off with fair words . . . He wants an army (of experts) all ready and complete . . . I don't know where they'll get the revolutionary spirit from. They're the same old clods (Prussian generals), and will certainly lose the next war.

Hitler did not see things like Röhm. He had already made it clear that he would need the skills of the highly trained Reichswehr if he were to build up stronger and larger armed forces. He also wanted this army led by powerful generals to support him if President Hindenburg died. Hitler intended to have Hindenburg's job as well as his own.

Hitler at first tried to persuade Röhm, but he and the SA leadership would not be bought off.

B Hitler's speech in the Reichstag, 13th July 1934

> I still had the secret hope that I might be able to spare my movement and my SA the shame of such disagreement and remove the mischief without severe conflict.

Hitler and other Nazi leaders came to see that the SA and Röhm would have to be dealt with by force. They chose a small group within the SA that had been set up by Goering and put under the control of Heinrich Himmler. This well trained special force was known as the SS (the protection squad).

On the morning of 30th June 1934, members of the SS drove to the place where Röhm and other SA leaders were meeting. The SA members were dragged from their beds and executed. There were several hundred other killings across Germany. Some were caused by revenge, some to wipe out opponents and some by mistake. . .

These killings became known as 'The Night of the Long Knives'.

C Extract from 'Inside the Third Reich' by Albert Speer, published 1970.

> When I saw Hitler on 1st July he was very excited . . . He kept describing how he too had forced his way into the SA hotel. He said, 'I alone was able to solve this problem. No-one else!' Hitler had menus of banquets held by Röhm, listing frog's legs, shark fins, expensive French wines. He said 'So, here we have these revolutionaries! And our revolution was too tame for them.'
>
> It was no accident that after this, the President, Minister of Justice and generals all lined up on Hitler's side. Hitler's action had wiped out the revolutionary left wing – there would be no 'second revolution' of the kind that Röhm was supposed to be plotting.

D President Hindenburg to Hitler after the killings, July 1934.

" ──────────────────────────

When circumstances require it, one must not shrink from the most extreme action. One must be able to spill blood also.

────────────────────────── "

Questions

1 In the early years of the Nazi party, Röhm and Hitler had been close friends. Using Sources **A** and **B**, explain why Hitler and Röhm were in disagreement by 1934.

2 **a** In Source C, Speer describes Hitler's reaction to what he found when the SA leadership were murdered. Explain Hitler's comments.

b Explain why Hitler was able to win over 'the President, Minister of Justice and generals'.

c Which sources indicate that President Hindenburg approved of the killings?

3 Source **E** is a British newspaper cartoon from 1934.

a Explain the 'joke' in the caption.

b How are Hitler, Goering and Goebbels shown?

c In which ways might the cartoon be called biased? Explain your answer carefully.

d How useful do you think cartoons are in telling us about events in the past?

E Cartoon about the Night of the Long Knives from a British newspaper in 1934.

Hitler   Goebbels   Goering

THEY SALUTE WITH BOTH HANDS NOW

Hitler's People

Hermann Goering (1893–1946)
Commander of fighter squadron in World War I; awarded highest award for bravery. Joined Nazi Party in 1922. Wounded in Munich Putsch 1923. Elected to Reichstag in 1928. President (Speaker) of the Reichstag in 1932. From 1933 became Interior Minister of Prussia. Built up the air force. Fat, vain, dependent on drugs. Took poison 1946.

Josef Goebbels (1897–1945)
Lame in one leg so could not fight in World War I. At first supported socialist wing of Nazi Party, but switched to Hitler in 1926. Built up Nazi support in Berlin 1926–30. Elected to Reichstag 1928 and 1930. Given control of Nazi propaganda machine before and after 1933. Brilliant propagandist, effective speaker.

Poisoned his six children and his wife before shooting himself 1945.

Heinrich Himmler (1900–1945)
Served in later part of World War I. Chicken farmer in Bavaria. Linked with Nazi Party from 1923. Hitler chose him in 1929 to create the SS (Schutz-Staffel = Protection Squad). Put in charge of Prussian secret police (Gestapo) in 1934 Later took control of all political police forces. Minister of the Interior from 1943. Responsible for the extermination and concentration camps. Committed suicide 1945.

Rudolf Hess (1894–1987)
Fought in World War I. Became Hitler's political secretary in 1920. Took part in Munich Putsch of 1923. Imprisoned with Hitler. Wrote down 'Mein Kampf' from Hitler's dictation. Became deputy leader of the Nazi Party in 1934. In 1941 he flew to Britain to try to make peace. Arrested and ignored. Sentenced in 1945 to life imprisonment. Died in Spandau Prison in Berlin in 1987.

The Perfect Citizen

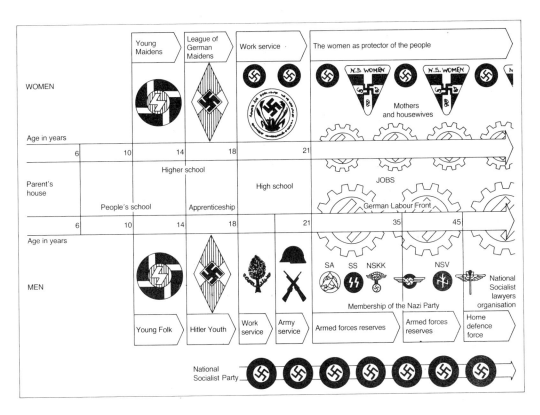

WOMEN			Young Maidens	League of German Maidens	Work service	The women as protector of the people		
Age in years	6	10	14	18	21			

Mothers and housewives

Parent's house			Higher school		High school	JOBS		
		People's school		Apprenticeship		German Labour Front		
Age in years	6	10	14	18	21	35	45	

| MEN | | | Young Folk | Hitler Youth | Work service | Army service | Armed forces reserves | Armed forces reserves | Home defence force |

SA SS NSKK NSV National Socialist lawyers organisation

Membership of the Nazi Party

National Socialist Party

A The way to become a perfect citizen.

The Nazis wanted to make every German follow the National Socialist way of doing things. They called this *Gleichschaltung* (meaning co-ordination) and the diagram (Source **A**) shows how they hoped the perfect citizen would live his or her life under Nazi rule.

B Robert Ley, head of the German Labour Front, quoted in 1944.

"

Our state is an educational state . . . It does not let a man go free from the cradle to the grave.

We begin with the child when he is three years old. As soon as he begins to think, he is made to carry a little flag. Then follows school, the Hitler Youth, the Storm Troopers and military training.

We don't let him go; when all is done, comes the Labour front, which takes over and does not let him go until he dies, even if he does not like it. ·

"

Here are three of Hitler's early views on the roles of men, women and children. All three sources are from his book, 'Mein Kampf'.

C Training of young men.

"

The present (Weimar) state does not interest itself in developing healthy men . . . The coming Peoples State will have to train young men after school in preparation for service in the army. The supreme task of the army will be to teach men to obey for both good and bad reasons.

D Views about women.

The German woman is a subject of the state, but becomes a citizen when she marries.

Young girls must get to know their sweethearts. If the beauty of the body was not hidden by our stupid manner of dress today, thousands of our girls would not be led astray by Jewish mongrels.

E Attitude to children.

Teachers should not encourage children to tell tales. A boy who tells on his friends is carrying out an act of treason. Such a boy should not be called 'good' or 'reliable'.

Children must be taught at an early age to suffer pain and injury without complaint. In the case of girls the final goal is to become a mother.

"

Workers and Work

The Nazis had come to power in 1933 promising work to the six million unemployed. The Communists had promised the same but by the middle of 1933 they had been wiped out as a political force. The last Centre Party government, led by Brüning, was blamed for doing nothing about the depression although this was not strictly true. All parties – apart from the two extreme ones on the left and right – were terrified of taking measures that might lead the economy straight back to the terrible days of the 1923 inflation. Moreover, there were powerful forces ranged against Brüning's government. When it did try to take action – for example by tackling the rights of rich landowners – the same landowners got to Hindenburg who in turn dismissed Brüning. Nevertheless, by 1932 something had been achieved by Brüning. The Allies at last agreed to phase out reparations, schemes had been drawn up by the government to start creating jobs and there were signs that the Depression was coming to an end.

These events were too late to save Brüning and it was Hitler who came to power just as unemployment began to fall.

A From Hitler's election speeches in February 1933.

❝

In fourteen years the Weimar System which has now been overthrown has piled mistake upon mistake.

I ask of you, German people, that after you have given the others fourteen years you should give us four.

What I claim is fair and just, only four years for us and then others shall judge us and pass sentence. I will not flee abroad, I will not seek to escape sentence.

❞

B Extract from an article by a member of the German Finance Ministry.

❝

After 1933, government policy aimed to keep wages low. The Trade Unions who might have fought for improvements were closed and replaced by the giant Nazi Labour Front which included both employers and workers. This was led by Dr Robert Ley, numbering some 25 million members ... Strikes were outlawed and any attempts usually severely punished. Labour laws usually favoured the employers ...

Nevertheless, most workers were satisfied that unemployment was falling. Total expenditure on work schemes of 5 billion marks, unemployed wiped 1½ million off the list by 1934. Construction also grew with government help. Re-armament also formed a part of the recovery plan ...

❞

C Extract from 'Germany Speaks' by Robert Ley.

❝

The main objects aimed at by the new Reich are:
1 The reduction of unemployment.
2 The build up of the materials needed to strengthen Germany's defences and her forces ...

❞

For the majority of the workforce, the peak year of the Depression, 1932, was fixed firmly in their minds. They did not compare their wages and conditions with the last pre-Depression year 1928. This was to help the Nazis as they repeatedly compared conditions and wages with 1932 in their propaganda.

D The government set many unemployed on public works projects such as building new motorways (the autobahns).

E Statistics of Germany economic recovery.

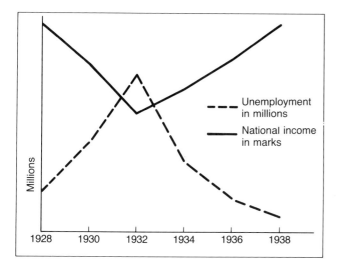

F Public spending 1928–1938 in billion marks.

	1928	1932	1933	1934	1935	1936	1937	1938
TOTAL SPENDING	23.2	17.1	18.4	21.6	21.9	23.6	26.9	37.1
CONSTRUCTION (houses, city plans etc.)	2.7	0.9	1.7	3.5	4.9	5.4	6.1	7.9
REARMAMENT (weapons, armed forces)	0.7	0.7	1.8	3.0	5.4	10.2	10.9	17.2
TRANSPORT (motorways, waterways)	2.6	0.8	1.3	1.8	2.1	2.4	2.7	3.8
OTHER WORK CREATION	–	0.2	1.5	2.5	0.8			

G Extract from 'Germany Speaks' by Robert Ley.

" ──────────

Special mention should be made here of a part of the German Labour Front – called 'Strength through joy' . . . The section for travelling and hiking is perhaps the most popular one . . . Its pleasure cruises to foreign countries have attracted great attention. Equally valuable have been tours within Germany . . . In 1934 some 2 million Germans had taken part, by 1936–6 million. The cost is low . . . Entertainment is provided . . . and another section tries to provide better conditions at work – e.g. baths, pools, canteens, open green spaces. . .

────────── "

Questions

1 What could Hitler have said in his pre-election speech in 1933 to justify:
   a His claim that the Weimar Governments had made many mistakes?
   b The workers in Germany would do better under the Nazi party.
2 Using the charts **E** and **F**, explain why the Nazis repeatedly compared wages and conditions under their government with 1932 figures and not 1928.
3 Dr Robert Ley led the Nazi Labour Front. Using Source **G** explain how:
   a he might have exaggerated his claims.
   b he might have been biased.
4 Draw a poster designed to promote 'Strength through joy' to German workers. (See Glossary.)

Women in Nazi Germany

A Adolf Hitler.

"

Woman is at all times the helper of man and thus his truest friend; while the man is at all times the protector of his wife and her best friend.

"

B From German Women to Adolf Hitler.

"

Men are grouped together in clubs and groups. Woman stays back further in the shadow of loneliness ... We see our daughters growing up in stupid aimlessness, living only in the vague hope of getting a man and having children. If they don't, their lives are ruined.

A son, even the youngest today, laughs in his mother's face. He sees her as his servant and women in general for his use.

"

C Frau Gertrud Scholtz-Klink the Nazi women's leader in 1938.

"

In 1933 we set up the Reich's Mother Service to train women. The object of such training is to teach them about their great duties: upbringing and education of their children and domestic and economic tasks.

"

D Dr Goebbels, Nazi propaganda chief.

"

Woman has the task of being beautiful and bringing children into the world, and this is by no means as old-fashioned as one might think. The female bird preens herself for her mate and hatches her eggs for him.

"

E A National Socialist Party poster saying that the Party ensures the togetherness of people in the community.

F The Mutterkreuz (or Mother Cross)

"

For outstanding service in the fight against a falling birth rate.
BRONZE = four children
SILVER = six children
GOLD = eight children

"

G The number of women employed in 1933, 1936 and 1939. ▶

H Advertisement.

> 52 year old doctor. Fought in World War I. Wishes to settle down. Wants male child through marriage to young, healthy Aryan woman. She should be undemanding, used to heavy work, not a spender, with flat heels, without earrings.

I German 'joke' in 1937.

> He who rules like a barbarian and imitates Napoleon, was born in Austria, trims his whiskers English-fashion, salutes like an Italian, makes German girls have children, but can't produce any himself – there's a German for you.

J German woman quoted in 'Hitler's Germany'.

> For years it was my fondest wish to see the Führer. I knew his voice from the radio. I saw his picture every day – on father's desk and on my wall next to my bed. I felt if I could see him but once I would be completely satisfied.
>
> But that was not true, for when I saw him in Munich, I wanted more. I wanted to see him close up: I wanted to hear him speak, to shake his hand. I wanted to tell him something, to thank him. But I would not have been able to say a word; like so many young and old, in those days, I would only have wept.

1933	11.48 million
1936	11.7 million
1939	12.7 million

K Hitler's secret mistress, Eva Braun

L Adolf Hitler.

> Lots of women are attracted to me because I'm unmarried. It's the same with a film star.

M Nazi newspaper, 1939.

> Only when the number of cradles exceeds the number of coffins can we look forward to a better future.

N 'Hitler's Table Talk', 1941.

> German girls have moulded themselves to the needs of the times – working in the war factories, the offices, the fields, the hospitals and so on.

Hitler Youth

When Hitler came to power in 1933 there were just over 100,000 members of the HJ – Hitler Jugend (Hitler Youth).

Almost at once, the Nazis began breaking up other youth groups. By 1939 only Catholic youth groups were left and they too were stopped in that year.

At first, membership of the HJ was voluntary but pressures were increasingly put on young people to join (although many *never* did).

The leader of the HJ was a 25 year old student called Baldur von Schirach. The leader of the female section of the HJ was Gertrud Scholtz-Klink. Baldur von Schirach was made Youth Leader of the Reich on 17th June 1933. He worked hard to build up the movement and on 1st December 1936 he was given permission to include all young Germans into the HJ and a new title of Supreme Reich Authority. By this time nearly 5½ million young people had joined the movement. Nearly a million HJ members took part in shooting competitions in 1938. By March 1939, all young Germans were called up to become members of the HJ.

Even before this final action was taken, the HJ was already the biggest youth movement seen in Germany and was one of the biggest in the world.

B Uniforms of the HJ and BdM.

A Structure of the youth movements.

> **Boys**
> 10–14 Jungvolk (JV) (Young folk). The boy was called a pimpf (cub).
> 14–18 Hitlerjugend (HJ) (Hitler Youth)
>
> **Girls**
> 10–14 Jungmädel (JM) (Young girls)
> 14–17 Bund deutscher Mädchen (BdM) (League of German Girls)
> 17–21 Voluntary membership of Glaube und Schönheit (Faith and Beauty)

C Hitler Youth Test.

"

To enter the JV or the JM children had to take tests at age 10. Below are some extracts from these tests:

Boys: Run 60 metres in 12 seconds,
Long jump 2.75 metres,
Throw a soft ball 25 metres,
Take part in a 36 hour hike.

Girls: Run 60 metres in 14 seconds,
Long jump 2 metres,
Throw a soft ball 12 metres,
Perform 2 somersaults forward and 2
backwards.

"

Achievements such as these were recorded in special 'Achievement Books'. These Service record books were to be kept from the age of 10 onwards.

D Cover of book given to each Hitler Youth member to record achievements.

LEISTUNGSBUCH DER HITLER-JUGEND

E A health and beauty display.

A Hitler Youth remembers

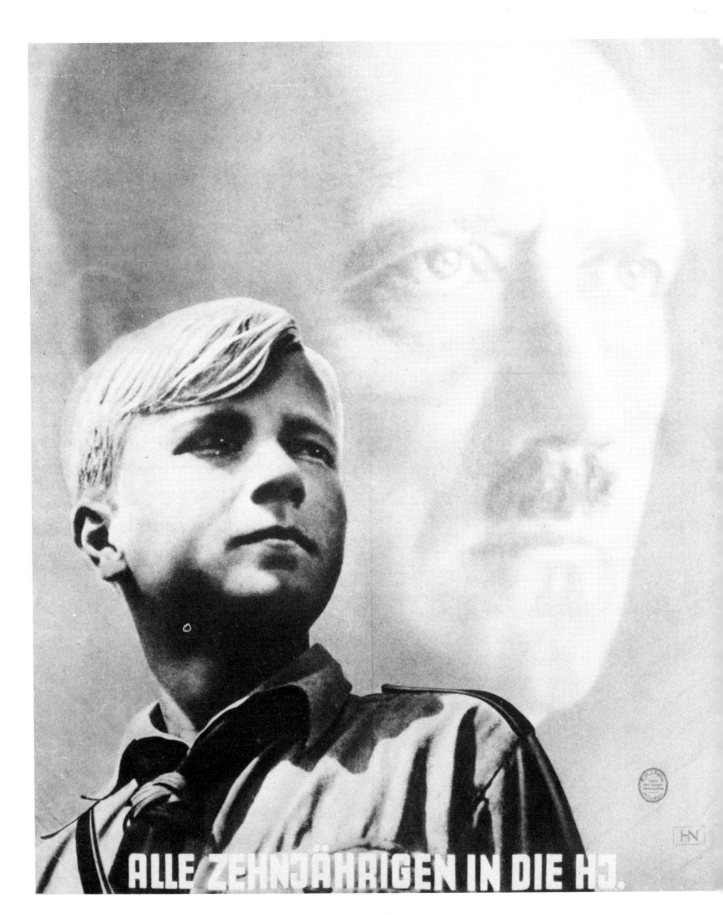

A A poster, entitled 'Youth Serve the Leader', said 'All ten year olds in the Hitler Youth.'

B Extracts from 'Hitler Youth' by, Hans Siemsen, published in 1940.

"

There were four of us in our family. My father was an engineer. My mother stayed at home to look after the house. There was my adopted brother and myself. We lived in a fairly large Rhineland town . . . Before Hitler there were already lots of youth movements. The patriotic Youth Movement was a pre-war organisation. The Wanderers, the Pathfinders, the order of Young Germans, the Catholic Leagues had all been set up after the war. Life in these groups was much the same – members went off on long hikes, held sing-songs, camped out, fought each other and so on. I know as I was a member of the Pathfinders. I knew almost nothing about politics. All I believed was that the Treaty of Versailles was unfair, that we had really won the war and that the only reason why things were going badly for us was that we had to pay expensive reparations to France . . .

A number of years passed while I trained as an athlete for the Olympic Games, but a smashed knee stopped that happening. However, when I tried to rejoin the Pathfinders I found that it had been banned by the Hitler government. In fact, of the groups I knew only the Catholic movement remained. There was now too the Hitler Youth . . . When I looked into the Hitler Youth I was told that it was completely unpolitical. I was told that any decent boy was welcome, that 'YOUTH STATES ITS OWN FUTURE' and 'THE COMMON GOOD BEFORE SELF INTEREST'. These slogans appealed to me!

"

"

My father tried to stop me joining but funnily enough it was pressure from my Jewish boss that made me join . . . He wanted, he said, to have a tame Nazi on his staff. As he would be forced to take one anyway he would rather it was me. So, I did, and the boss even paid for my whole uniform . . . At my first parade I clattered through my quiet neighbourhood in my new boots. I felt a little embarrassed but very proud as neighbours peered from their windows . . .

"

C Hitler Youth bugle.

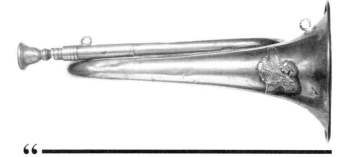

"

I may as well confess right here that I took part in everything and what I did not take part in myself I knew about and let happen by not saying anything. I didn't think there was anything wrong in it. I just joined in, did what everyone seemed to be doing. I joined in the hope of living a friendly, happy life according to Hitler's ideas – had he not said 'You boys, members of the Hitler Youth, you are the guarantees of the future'?

"

"

Here are some of the rules told to me by the HJ Troop Leader.
1 Members of the HJ must not be seen in uniform with girls.
2 HJ members must ignore friends and parents whilst marching along.
3 Members must not buy things at Jewish shops.
We sang songs as we marched. Here are two excerpts:
'We shall fight and beat the French and like gallant heroes die'.
'When Jewish blood spurts from the knife, then everything will be fine'.
When we weren't marching we threw hand grenades with blank charges and did other military exercises. Before Hitler took over there were only 200 members of the HJ in our town. Within a few months there were 3,000.

"

"

Growing dissatisfied with the ways of the HJ, I formed my own small group. I was brought before the Regional Leader. He said, 'I know all about you. You go about in civilian clothes. You go on hikes . . . But you can't do that these days. We have to fight . . . We have to prepare for the day of reckoning, for the great struggle between the nations. Is Germany to go under in that fight?

"

Assignment: Hitler Youth

The purpose of this material is to look at the varied experiences of young people during the Nazi period and attempt to reconstruct their different responses to the pressures, values and events of that period.

While you are thinking about this subject, try to avoid *anachronism*, that is putting an event, person or thing into a historical description in which it could not have occurred or existed. For example, a person in the Stone Age wearing a Roman soldier's clothes or a Roman soldier watching TV.

Try also to avoid *stereotyping*, that is assuming that the same type of person always acts in the same way in given situations. For example, assuming that young people are always rude and untidy, all old people complain all the time or all football fans are hooligans.

The chapters you should read are on pages 52 to 55, but you will find evidence in other parts of the book (don't forget the glossary on pages 92–95) and in other books too.

Questions

1 Look at the diagram (Source A) on page 47 about the perfect citizen.
   a What routes are mapped out for children in that diagram? Start from the birth of the child and note down at what ages they are expected to change.
   b What differences can you see in the life plans for boys and girls?
   c Account for these differences by using the evidence in the chapters dealing with men, women and children.
2 Read the chapter on Women. Then answer these questions.
   a What were the Nazi's views on the role of women?
   b Can you explain why the numbers of working women remained high throughout the Nazi period and actually increased towards the end?
   c Note down any evidence you can find that shows that not all German women agreed with Nazi views on the role of women.
3 Read the chapters on Hitler Youth and A Hitler Youth Remembers (pages 52–55). Then answer these questions.
   a Why did so many young people volunteer to join the Hitler Youth?
   b In what ways were the activities different from those of other youth groups in Germany?

   c The boy in the A Hitler Youth Remembers chapter is never named. Why might he not have wanted to have his name revealed in the book?
   d Explain why the Jewish boy's boss paid for him to join the Hitler Youth.
   e Is there any evidence in the sources that the boy was anti-Jewish? If not, why did he join in the songs about the Jews?
   f How did the boy and his friends later react to the Hitler Youth? How different were their activities from those of the Hitler Youth?
   g What evidence is there that not joining the Hitler Youth became more difficult as the Nazis' control of power grew in Germany?
4 a Is there any evidence in these chapters and the chapter on Education (page 57) that boys and girls received different treatment at school?
   b Subject emphasis changed in most schools. History, German and games increased; religious education decreased. Can you explain these changes?
5 In which ways did Hitler succeed in encouraging, or making, young people learn Nazi ideas and join the Hitler Youth Movement? Although many did not join, why was it difficult to refuse?

Education

The German state education system had been set up in the nineteenth century. It had been given much of the credit for the spectacular events that had led to the unification of Germany under Prussian rule in 1871. Many teachers of that time were strong nationalists and this tradition continued into the present century.

After Germany's defeat in the First World War, large numbers of teachers made it clear to their pupils that the new Weimar Republic was a betrayal of all that was best in Germany. The consequent rise in power of the National Socialists was welcomed by the majority of teachers. 97 per cent of the profession joined the new Nazi Teachers Association and large numbers joined the party itself.

There was therefore little need for the Nazi government to make major changes in the school system at first.

However, this is not to say that adjustments were not made where it was thought necessary to spread Nazi ideas as soon as possible. They set up special schools for a few whom the Nazis believed would turn out to be the new generation of leaders. These Napolas (National Political Institutes of Education) were run by ex-members of the SS. Athletics and general courage were what those in control were looking for. Academic ability was less important. Boys who wore glasses were not admitted! Later, the Nazis built four Ordensburgen (Castles of Order) where men who had already done their military service were trained to become the new leaders of Nazi Germany.

C The timetable from the girls' school.

A Boys at a special Nazi training school.

B A visit to a Nazi girls' school, recorded in 'Education for Death' by Gregor Ziemer in 1942.

> The school bell called the girls . . . before I visited the classes I spoke to the head teacher. She told me that every class in the school was built around a course called 'Activities of Women'. This course was divided into handwork, domestic science, cooking, house and garden work – and the most important section – breeding and hygiene. This section dealt with sex education, birth, childcare . . .

PERIODS	MONDAY	TUESDAY	WEDNESDAY	THURSDAY	FRIDAY	SATURDAY
1. 8:00 – 8:45	GERMAN	GERMAN	GERMAN	GERMAN	GERMAN	GERMAN
2. 8:50 – 9:35	GEOGRAPHY	HISTORY	SINGING	GEOGRAPHY	HISTORY	SINGING
3. 9:40 – 10:25	RACE STUDY	RACE STUDY	RACE STUDY	RACE STUDY	PARTY BELIEFS	PARTY BELIEFS
4. 10:25 – 11:00	BREAK — WITH SPORTS AND SPECIAL ANNOUNCEMENTS					
5. 11:00 – 12:05	DOMESTIC SCIENCE WITH MATHEMATICS — EVERY DAY					
6. 12:10 – 12:55	THE SCIENCE OF BREEDING (EUGENICS) – HEALTH BIOLOGY				2:00 – 6:00 SPORT EACH DAY	

D From a children's book of the period. The words say: Who wants to be a soldier must have a gun; He must load it with powder and a heavy bullet; Kiddie, if you want to be a recruit, take note of this song.

E A school problem from 'Other Men's Graves' by Peter Neumann, published in 1958.

" ———

When Klaus got home from school he bullied me into helping him with his homework . . . here is a maths problem picked out at random, 'A pilot on take off carries 12 bombs, each weighing 10 kilos. The plane flies to Warsaw (the capital of Poland and centre for Jews). It bombs the town. On take off with all bombs on board and a fuel tank containing 1,500 kilos of fuel, the aircraft weighed about eight tons. When it returned from the crusade there are still 230 kilos of fuel left. What is the weight of the aircraft when empty?'

——— "

F A German newspaper on education 1939.

" ———

All subjects – German language, history geography, chemistry and mathematics – must concentrate on military subjects. They must glory in military service, German heroes and leaders and the strength of the new Germany . . .

——— "

G How the teachers' newspaper saw education in 1939.

" ———

The general aims of school education are
1 Increasing physical fitness for military service.
2 Providing the necessary knowledge and practical efficiency in preparation for military service

——— "

Questions

1 Complete the following flow chart:

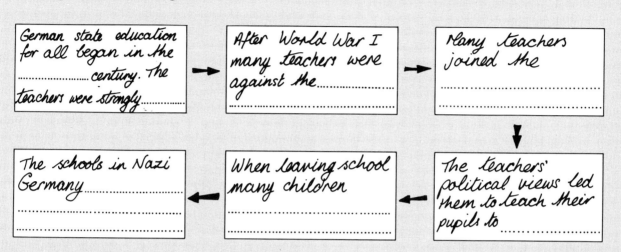

German state education for all began in the .... century. The teachers were strongly ....

→

After World War I many teachers were against the ....

→

Many teachers joined the ....

↓

The teachers' political views led them to teach their pupils to ....

←

When leaving school many children ....

←

The schools in Nazi Germany ....

2 Look at Source **A**.
  a What do you think that the boys in the picture are doing?
  b Explain why you think they were put through tests of this kind?
3 Sources **B** and **C** are about education for girls.
  a In which ways do they reflect the ideal Nazi woman? (You may need to re-read the chapter on Women.)
  b Read Source **F**. Explain which subjects were taught to both boys and girls.
4 **a** Read the maths problem in Source **E** and explain why someone who was anti-Nazi might have felt alarmed at reading such a question.

  b Invent your own maths problem that would have been acceptable in a Nazi maths text book.
5 How did the Napolas fulfil the general aims as set out in Source **G**?

Follow-on question

6 'Nazi Education was based on brainwashing.'
  a Using all the sources, find evidence to support this statement.
  b Explain in what way you may be using hindsight (being wise after the event) to answer this question.

Nazis and Christians

Germany had (and still does have) important religious divisions dating back hundreds of years to the Reformation. North German Christians are usually Protestant, while those in the south remain Catholic. Hitler himself was born a Catholic and there is no evidence that he ever gave up the faith. Both Catholic and Protestant church leaders had found much to dislike in the new Weimar Republic. Both disapproved of a Republic that said that religion should be separate from the work of government. The Nazi movement and its success from 1933 posed even greater problems for the two churches. The Protestants were not very well organised and this left them open to Nazi influence. The Catholics were much better prepared, but they knew that they might be criticised as being un-German by the Nazis who might say they were getting their 'orders' from the Pope in Rome.

The Catholics came to terms with the Nazis very quickly in order to hang on to some of their educational/social freedoms. In June 1933 a Concordat (understanding) was agreed. The Pope in the Vatican recognised Hitler's government as the 'real' government of Germany. As for the Protestants many supported the choice of Ludwig Müller as 'Reichsbishop' in September 1933 believing that the appointment would bring Nazis and Protestants closer together, but it only lasted two years. In 1935, Hitler set up a new 'Department for Church Affairs' which began to interfere in church life.

Many Nazis hated Christianity completely. They attacked the faith and said that it had been replaced by a superior religion – that of National Socialism itself. Hitler was the new Messiah and his followers the new disciples.

A A Hitler Youth song sung at the Nuremburg Nazi Party rally in 1934.

"

No evil priest can stop us feeling that we are the children of Hitler. We follow not Christ, but Horst Wessel (a Nazi stormtrooper killed in a fight and now turned into a hero and subject of one of the Nazis' favourite tunes). Away with incense and holy water. The Church can go hang for all we care. The Swastika brings salvation on earth . . .

"

B Nazi propaganda made much of meetings with church leaders. Hitler is told by the Pope's representative that he now understands the Nazi movement.

C In the Protestant town of Wittenberg at a meeting of the German evangelical national synod Ludwig Müller is hailed as Reichsbishop on 27th September 1933.

D **Dictation passage for a Junior School pupil in 1933.**

" Just as Jesus freed mankind from sin so Hitler saves the German people from destruction . . . The apostles completed the work of their Lord. We hope that Hitler will be able to complete his own work. Jesus built for Heaven, Hitler for the German earth. "

E **Hitler on Christianity in his 'Table Talk', December 1941.**

" The war will be over one day. I shall then see my life's final task as solving the religious problem . . . Our people has managed to live without religion before . . . I have six SS divisions made up of men without any religion . . . It doesn't stop them going to their deaths with peace in their souls . . . Christianity is an invention of sick brains. "

F **Pastor Martin Niemoller, June 1937.**

" Heaven help us if we made a German Gospel out of the Gospel, a German church out of Christ's church, German Christians out of Evangelical Christians "

Questions

1 Explain carefully how photographs like **B** and **C** might persuade the ordinary people in Germany that the Protestant and Catholic churches approved of and supported the Nazi Party.
2 What evidence can you find in the text and from source **E** that one day Hitler intended to get rid of all Christian activities?
3 In most religions you can identify certain common features. Which of the following features can you see in Nazi beliefs? Explain where you get your evidence from. Fill in the chart below to sort out your answers.
   a A messenger from God.
   b Saints and Martyrs.
   c A Holy Book.
   d A symbol or special sign.
   e Songs or hymns.
   f Followers.

Common feature	Christian Church	Nazi ideas	Evidence to support
a b c d e Songs/Music	Hymns Religious Songs	Hitler Youth Song	Source **A** song sung at a Nüremberg rally – the Horst Wessel song.
f			

Propaganda

In 'Mein Kampf' Hitler made it clear that he believed that propaganda was vital if the Nazis were to succeed. He had been impressed by what he saw as the major part played by British propaganda in Germany's defeat in the First World War. He had also studied the use of propaganda by political parties in Vienna before the First World War.

Propaganda for Hitler was a way of gaining and keeping the support of the masses. To that end, it was necessary to keep the messages and slogans as simple as possible. These slogans should be repeated over and over again. It did not matter whether the message was a complete lie. In fact the bigger the lie the better. If said often and boldly enough at least part of it would be believed.

These beliefs were taken up and developed by Dr Josef Goebbels whom Hitler made his Minister for Propaganda and Enlightenment of the People in 1933. Goebbels made full use of every opportunity to spread the Nazi message. Posters, flags, gramophone records of speeches, toys, newspapers, radio, cinema and great public meetings/rallies were all used by Goebbels and his ministry.

A Nazi holidays.

"

As soon as they came to power, the Nazis brought in a number of festivals.

Jan 30th   Day of seizure of power.
Feb 24th   Nazi party founded.
Mar 10th   National Heroes' Remembrance Day
Apr 20th   Hitler's birthday.
May 1st   National Day of Labour.
May   Mothering Sunday.
Jun   Day of the Summer Solstice.
Sep   Harvest Thanksgiving.
Sep   Party Rally at Nuremberg.
Nov 9th   Munich Putsch Anniversary.
Dec   Day of the Winter Solstice.

"

B Hitler touches the Blood Flag from 1923, an SA standard, at the Nuremberg Rally in 1929.

C Hitler on propaganda.

"

The art of propaganda consists . . . in being able to awaken the imagination of the public through an appeal to their feelings . . Its chief function is to convince the masses; whose slowness of understanding needs to be given time in order that they may absorb information, and only constant repetition will finally succeed in imprinting the idea on the memory of the crowd.

"

D William Shirer, an American reporter, 1934.

"

Like a Roman Emperor, Hitler rode into this . . . town . . . past . . . wildly cheering Nazis who packed the narrow streets . . . the streets are a sea of brown and black uniforms . . . About 10 o'clock I got caught in a mob of ten thousand hysterics who jammed the moat in front of Hitler's hotel shouting, 'We want our Führer' . . . They looked up at him as if he were the Son of God . . .

"

E Scene at a Nazi rally. ▶

F Albert Speer, the chief decorator at the Nazi rallies, describes how the scene was set and why.

"

(After a few years in power) it was clear that some of the old Nazis had developed sizeable beer guts. (At the rallies) it was difficult to present them in a good light. Suddenly the answer came to me 'Let's have them march in darkness' . . .

I asked Hitler to let me have 130 searchlights to blaze directly into the sky at intervals of 12 metres. They reached 10,000 metres into the sky.

"

G Neville Henderson, the British Ambassador to Germany, describes a Nazi rally.

"

. . . Hitler himself arrived at the far end of the stadium, some 400 yards (130 metres) from the platform . . . His arrival was (signalled) by the sudden turning into the air of 300 or more searchlights with which the stadium was surrounded. The blue tinged light from these met thousands of feet up in the sky at the top to make a kind of square roof, to which a chance cloud gave added realism. The effect . . . was like being in a cathedral of ice.

"

H William Shirer describes the rallies.

"

After seven days of almost ceaseless goose-stepping, speechmaking and pageantry, the Party rally came to an end tonight. You have to go through one of these (rallies) to understand Hitler's hold on the people . . . And now – as Hitler told us yesterday . . . the half million men who've been here during the week will go back to their towns and villages and preach the new gospel with new fanaticism.

"

Questions

1 Using Source **A,** what festivals are similar to those in the Christian church? Which are completely different? Explain carefully.
2 'If nothing else Hitler was a great showman.' Use the evidence in **E, F** and **G** to illustrate this view.
3 In the chapter on religion Hitler was described as a 'Messiah'.
   a How is he described in Source **D** by Shirer?
   b What does this tell us about Hitler's power and means of keeping his power? (Use the glossary if you do not understand reference to the brown and black uniforms.)
   c Do you think Shirer admires or dislikes Hitler? Give clear reasons (Source **H**).

Follow-on questions

4 Using the text and Source **H,** explain in what ways spreading the Nazi message compared with an Evangelical Church which wants to spread the word of God?
5 Explain why we have a good deal of foreign pro-Hitler propaganda dating from 1933–38, but that after 1939 it is nearly all critical.

German Cinema

Even before Hitler came to power, many film directors in Weimar Germany had been making films of which the Nazis approved. These were largely the work of the pro-Hitler Nationalist Party leader, Alfred Hugenberg. Besides controlling a large number of newspapers, Hugenberg owned the Universal Film Company (UFA). UFA was the biggest producer of films in Germany. Hugenberg's support of Hitler meant that he remained in charge of UFA when the Nazis took over.

This did not please Goebbels (the propaganda minister) who had to be content with influencing the work of the film makers. He did this by setting up a special office in his ministry through which all plans for new films had to pass.

This film office first checked the script to see if it was acceptable. Then the directors and performers were checked to make sure that none of them were Jews or enemies of the Nazis. Films were then checked as they were being made and, when finished, checked again by the censors.

Goebbels knew that the cinema-goers would soon get fed up with too many obviously political films. In the twelve years that the Nazis were in power, they produced about 1150 films. Only some 200 of these were direct political propaganda.

Goebbels preferred to have political films as special events. He also knew that the Nazis could put their views across to every cinema-goer every week by using the cinema news film programme.

Cinema in the Third Reich suffered as Nazi race policies drove talented Jews and political opponents abroad to pursue their careers.

B Review: Dawn 1933

"

In the central scene of the film, the submarine sinks. There is escape apparatus for only 8 out of 10 men. The men refuse to leave the two officers who have volunteered to die, saying 'All or none'. The Captain says, 'Such men! I could die ten deaths for Germany – no, one hundred.' Then, 'Perhaps we Germans don't understand life very well, but we have a wonderful understanding of death – we will stay as a team in death.' In the end two men kill themselves to save the others.

"

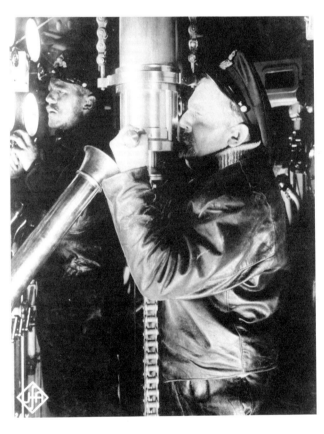

A Review: The Eternal Jew 1940

"

The film opens with these words, 'We in Germany know the civilised Jews, but they give us only part of the racial picture. This film, shot in the Polish Ghettos, shows us Jews as they really are: cunning, cowardly, inhuman and horrible, flocking together in great herds. As with rats, Jews mix with and live by ordinary people.'

"

C Review: Kolberg 1945

"

Named after a German town that refused to surrender to Napoleon's French in 1806, Kolberg is about one man, Nettleback, who begs the army commander to fight on. 'You were not born in Kolberg, Commander, but we grew up here. We know every stone and corner. Better to be buried under the ruins than surrender. I beg you on my knees: don't surrender the town.'

"

D Review: Hitler Youth Quex 1933

"

The brave little hero dies a soldier's death: for his cause, for his comrades, for his beloved flag and his leader. But other German youths again raise the flag high – now heavy with the blood of one of the best.

"

E Visits to the cinema in Germany

"

1932/3	238 million
1935	317 million
1939	623.7 million
1943	1129 million

"

F Excerpts from conversations of film-goers overheard and reported by secret police officers and informers.

"

Quite interesting, but in this film (Mercy Killing), the same thing happens as in the insane asylums where they are finishing the lunatics all off right now! What guarantee have we got that no abuse creeps in?

'Typical dirty Jew.'

'Usual Jewish hooligan.'

'Serve Jew Süss right. They should hang all of them.'

The film The Great King (on the life of Frederick the Great) led the audience to say that this is a mirror image of our own times. Many have compared the King with Hitler.

"

Questions

1 Source **E** shows the number of visits to the cinema made by Germans in the period 1932–43. How do you explain the increase in the number of visits?
2 Compare the reviews in sources **B** and **D** of the two films. What similarities are there in their treatment of
   a Death.
   b Germans?
3 Source **F**, contains secret police reports.
   a Why do you think the police were told to listen to comments made by cinema-goers?
   b Which comments would come closest to pleasing the Nazis?
   c Which comments might have displeased the Nazis?

Follow-on questions

4 The text says that out of 1,150 films made in the Nazi period, only some 200 were direct political propaganda. Why do you think this was?
5 Explain how the Nazis might have hoped to influence the behaviour of ordinary Germans through the films described here.
6 What methods might be used today to put across a propaganda message?

The Arts

Germany's reputation in the Arts had been growing even before World War I. In 1919 the Bauhaus School of Design was started in Weimar. The Bauhaus movement included artists like Schlemmer and Klee as well as architects, furniture makers, sculptors and designers. In 1925 the group moved to Messau and in 1930 to Berlin. It was closed by the Nazis in 1933. The Bauhaus was only part of the huge development of all of the arts in the 1920s in Germany. Museums were full of modern art, new operas were written such as the 'Threepenny Opera' by Berthold Brecht and composer Kurt Weill, and the cinema used advanced techniques.

In 1929, the Nazis set up the Militant League for German Culture. This organisation staged demonstrations against 'modern art', for example they staged riots at Weill's new opera and outside the anti-war film 'All Quiet on the Western Front'. Schlemmer's wall paintings were white-washed out at the Bauhaus. Any art that was thought to be non-Aryan, Communist or anti-war was banned.

Nazi art was told to feature the hero and heroine, to be 'true to life' and to support Nazi ideas about war, family and community. Books and pictures that did not do this were destroyed, in the book burnings in Berlin (10th May 1933), as were 5,000 paintings in 1936. All the Arts were put under the control of Goebbels' Propaganda Ministry. Writers were stopped from writing, painters from painting, etc. Many fled abroad. Hitler also had strong ideas about architecture.

B An acceptable Nazi subject for a painting.

A Hitler's architect, Albert Speer, plans for the new Berlin on Hitler's order.

"

I went to Hitler's once or twice a week around midnight after the last film had been run . . . As the other guests withdrew we talked about his ruling passion. His favourite project was our model city set up in the nearby Berlin Academy of Arts. He had had special doors put in to link it with the Chancellery . . . Illuminated by spotlights, the models were kept under close guard. No one was allowed to see the grand plan for the rebuilding of Berlin without Hitler's permission . . . My father came to see the model. He only shrugged his shoulders and said, 'You've all gone completely crazy' . . .

•   •   •

The great avenue between the two central railway stations was meant to spell out the power of Germany . . . In the centre sat the absolute ruler of the Reich, and by him the greatest expression of his power, the great domed hall. This would be able to hold 180,000 people. The dome would reach a height of 746 feet . . . from the outside the dome would have looked like a green mountain as it was to be roofed in copper sheets. At the peak would be a turret 136 feet high. The turret would be crowned by an eagle with a swastika in its claws . . . One day in early 1939 Hitler told me, 'That has to be changed. Instead of the swastika, the eagle is to be perched above the globe . . .'

"

C Nazi architecture: The principal arena in Nuremburg, 1936.

Questions

1 Suggest four subjects for painting that Hitler would have approved of, and four subjects that he would have banned.
2 Account for Hitler's attitude to architecture and art under the following headings:
   a He wanted to become an art student.
   b He wanted to construct grand buildings in Nazi Germany.
   c He wanted to influence all aspects of German people's lives.
   d He disliked the 'Weimar art' and preferred traditional 'Folk art'.
3 Draw your own plan or sketch to illustrate the second part of Speer's description of the new capital.

4 Read through the information in this chapter again.
   Do you think Hitler encouraged art and literature in all its forms? Explain your answer carefully.
5 Why do you think that Hitler ordered the changing of the eagle gripping a swastika to that perched above the globe in early 1939?

Follow-on question

6 What might anti-Nazis have said about the Nazi style of art and literature?

Sport

A Nazi view on sport by Hans Tchammer ünd Osten, Sports Leader of Germany in 1938.

"

When Hitler asked me, in 1933, to become leader of German Sports, the conditions that I found were very bad indeed. On the one hand was a people anxious to take part in physical exercise, on the other a narrow minded system that couldn't provide the necessary back up . . . Since 1900 sport had become far too specialised. Each type of sport had set itself up on its own. There were hundreds of local clubs, district associations and regional associations for each sport. There was no central organisation directing the sports activities of the whole nation . . . The fact that such a central organisation was set up and was behind the universally acknowledged successes of the 1936 Olympic Games proves to the world the success of these methods. These are backed by the army, the Hitler Youth local councils, schools and their teachers. Together we will make sure that we will all work together for all time.

"

B Hitler on the Olympic Games from his 'Table Talk', 1942.

"

At the time when it was decided that the Olympic Games should be held here, the Ministry gave several plans to me for the building of a new stadium. None of these (penny pinching) schemes seemed to take into account . . . that we had here the splendid chance to build up our prestige abroad.

"

C Ambition in the Hitler Youth by Hans Siemsen, 1940

"

In 1932 the athletics club decided to have me trained for the 1936 Games. I decided to go in for an athletic career to be an Olympic champion and after that to be a teacher of athletics . . .

"

D How Hitler used the 1936 Olympic Games as recorded by Albert Speer in his 'Inside the Third Reich'.

"

Hitler gave orders that everything should be done to give foreign guests the impression that they were in a peace loving Germany.

"

E Hitler on the future of the Olympics reported by Albert Speer.

"

In 1937, Hitler and I talked about the new stadium he had decided to build in Berlin. As we looked at my scale model I pointed out that my athletics field was not the same as the Olympic proportions. He said, 'No matter. In 1940 the next Olympic Games will take place in Tokyo. After that they will take place in Germany in this stadium for all time . . . and we will decide the rules.'

"

F The 1936 Olympic Games from John Toland's 'Hitler', 1976.

"

That summer of 1936 the Olympics were staged in Berlin despite efforts by anti-Nazis in Britain, the U.S. and France to get people to stay away because of anti-semitism. Some Jews had been allowed to take part in the events and one had been put in charge of the Olympic village (where the athletes lived). Anti-Jewish signs (e.g. 'Jews not wanted here') disappeared as did anti-Jew newspapers . . .

Hitler opened the Games on 1st August, in the world's largest stadium . . . A special 'Olympic Hymn' composed by world famous German composer Richard Strauss was played by an orchestra and sung by a chorus of 3,000.

The crowd of 110,000 now cheered the marchpast of the teams. Some foreign teams gave the Nazi salute. Neither the British nor American teams raised their arms although the French did . . . The whole games were filmed by Leni Riefenstahl and the film made widely available.

"

G Hitler on race and the Olympics as reported by Albert Speer.

“

Hitler himself followed the athletic contests with great excitement . . . but he was highly annoyed by the successes of the black American runner, Jesse Owens. Hitler said that such people had an unfair advantage over civilised white people as they were descended from jungle primitives. They were unfair competition and would be excluded from future games.

”

H Jesse Owens, the American black Olympic runner reported in Toland's 'Hitler'.

“

When I passed the Chancellor (Hitler) he got up, waved his hand at me, and I waved back at him. I think the writers showed bad taste in criticizing the man of the hour.

”

I The German torch bearer runs past the crowd to light the Olympic flame on the first day of the 1936 Olympics.

J Results of the Games

Gold medals:	Germany	33
	USA	57
	Britain	8

Questions

1 a What problems does Hans Tchammer report in Source **A** when he took over control of German sport?
  b What successes does he claim to have had?
  c How are these successes illustrated in Source **J**?
  d Why was Hitler so keen to improve German sport?

2 Using Sources **B** and **D**.
  a Explain what two effects on foreign opinion Hitler hoped to achieve by holding the Olympic Games in Berlin.
  b Do you think his aims are the same or different from those of host countries in recent years? Explain your answer carefully.

3 How could you use the evidence in Source **E** to predict Hitler's future plans?

4 Look back at the chapter on Propaganda (pages 62–63) before answering these questions.
  a How does Source **F** add to the view that Hitler was a showman?
  b In Source **I** how would you be able to identify this as the Berlin Olympics of 1936?

5 Comparing Sources **G** and **H**, what do you consider to be similar and different? Which of the two pieces of evidence do you think is the more reliable? Explain carefully.

69

Nazi ideas on race

The belief that there were recognisable races and that these races were in some sort of order with the so-called Aryan race at the top influenced life a great deal in Nazi Germany. You will find detailed examples of these ideas on p. 32 in the section called Prison and the Book and in the whole section on the Jews – pp. 70–80.

As you may have noticed in the section on Education in Nazi Germany p. 57, these ideas on race were taught in schools. There are several other pieces of evidence from schools in these pages.

The belief that life was a struggle and that only the fittest survived was not invented by Hitler and the Nazis. It had grown out of the works of a nineteenth century scientist called Charles Darwin. He had put forward the theory of *Evolution*. Darwin claimed that all the existing varieties of plants and animals, including man, far from having been the same since the beginning of time, had come into being through a series of changes. Others then took Darwin's ideas and looked at just human beings. They called their theory *Social Darwinism*. This new theory was popular at the end of the nineteenth and in the early twentieth century. It said that it was the law of nature that the strongest 'race' would beat the weaker ones, and eventually rule the world.

A **Hitler on the Jews in 'Mein Kampf', 1924.**

" What soon gave me cause for alarm were the Jews at work. Was there any shady undertaking, any form of foulness, especially in cultural life, in which at least one Jew did not take part? "

B **Nazi Race book 1929.**

" The Nordic (Aryan) race is tall, long-legged, slim . . . male height of above 1.74 m. This race is narrow faced . . . with a narrow forehead, a narrow high-built nose and a lower narrow jaw and prominent chin . . . the skin is rosy bright and the blood shines through . . . the hair is smooth straight or wavy – possibly curly in childhood. The colour is blond . . . and this colour can be seen as a sign of some Nordic influence in other nearby races . . . "

C **Hitler to his Commanders in Chief in November 1939.**

" . . . I see struggle as the fate of all living creatures. No one can escape it, unless he wishes to be defeated. The increasing numbers of our people need more space. It was my aim to bring about a more sensible balance between space and population. That must be the starting part of the struggle . . . "

D **The SS view of the Jews in 1935 reported by Walther Hofer in 1957.**

" The greatest enemy of earth conquering man is man himself. The sub-human *seems* like us; with arms, hands, feet, a kind of brain, eyes and a mouth. In reality it is a quite different, fearful creature – a rough sketch of a human being, but in mind and soul lower than the lowest animal. In the heart of this creature lies a terrible urge for destruction. AND THE UNDERWORLD OF THE SUB-HUMANS FOUND ITS LEADER – THE ETERNAL JEW. "

E **School work on race from 'Race Biology for Pupils', 1935.**

"
1 Collect example from stories, essays and poems of the individual races.
2 What are the expressions, gestures, and movements which allow us to recognise different races?
3 Determine the race according to physical characteristics. Repeat this exercise with the pictures of great men of all nations and times.
4 Observe the Jew: his way of walking, his bearing, gestures, and movements when talking.
"

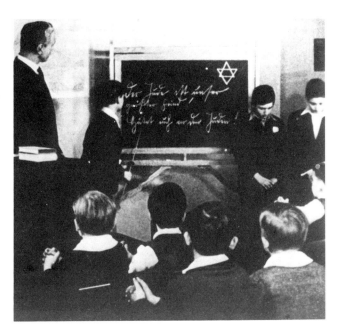

G Jewish boys used as an example in class.

F The 'true' Aryan pupil used as a class example.

H Anti-Jewish poster entitled 'The Eternal Jew' for a 'political exhibition' held in the German Museum of Munich in November 1937.

Questions

1 In what ways do Sources **D** and **H** attack Jews?
2 Which theory in the main text does Hitler seem to be describing in Source **C**?
3 In Source **F** and **G** children are being used as examples in class. What do you think might be being said about then?
4 **a** In Source **H**, what is the Jew carrying under his arm? What does it represent?
  b Explain what he is holding in his hands.
  c What do you think was the purpose of the picture (other than as a poster)?

The Jews: the background

In 63 BC, the Jewish homeland of Judea was taken over by the Roman Empire. Rebellions by the Jews in AD 70 and AD 132 failed. Many Jews left Judea and spread out throughout the Roman Empire. They were usually allowed to follow their religion and played a full part in most areas of Roman life.

However, when the Romans became officially Christians in the fourth century the position of the Jews worsened. Over the next few hundred years they were driven out of some areas, forbidden to own land, their property taken away from them.

In the tenth/eleventh century Jews set up towns in the Rhine valley in Germany. Others went even further into Poland. Here the Jews spoke their own language based on German. It became known to the rest of the world later as Yiddish.

Jews were already labelled with the title of 'Christ killers'. They now suffered because their religion allowed them to lend money and charge interest. At this time the Christian Church was against this. The Christian Church spoke out against the Jews. As a result Jews were made to pay fines for no reason, wear badges (often yellow) and forced to live in certain areas and banned in others.

A Jews out of England from Chambers' 'Book of Days', 1879.

> When King Edward I of England returned he found the whole nation had become in debt to the Jews. On the 31st August 1290 Edward commanded that all persons of the Jewish race must leave England by 1st November or they would be killed. They were allowed to take a small amount of what they owned, but the people rose and robbed the Jews on all sides.

B Log book of the Berlin guard in 1743 on the day the Jews were allowed to return to the city.

> Today there passed through the Rosenthal Gate six oxen, seven pigs, one Jew.

C Jews out of Europe.

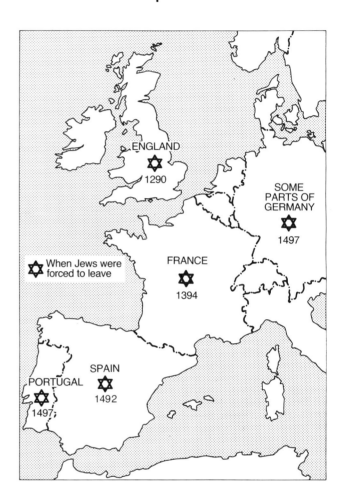

D The Jews in Frankfurt.

> In 1929 the number of Jews living in the large German industrial and trading city of Frankfurt was about 30,000 or roughly 5.5 per cent of the population of 540,000. It was the second largest Jewish community in Germany after Berlin.
>
> At the beginning of the 19th century Jews were no longer expected to live in the ghetto, and the law declared them equal. Their new legal position began to make it easier for them to play a full part in the development of the city. Although anti-semitism never fully disappeared, Frankfurt was – for the most part – a tolerant city. Jews had the chance to keep their traditional way of life or join into society at large.

E Frankfurt synagogue, built in 1882.*

*A synagogue is a Jewish church.

F Jews Street, Frankfurt's Jewish ghetto.
Before the nineteenth century the street was closed every night and non-Jews were not allowed to enter.

G The Kolnerhof Hotel near Frankfurt railway station, 1905.
The sign says 'Jewish visitors forbidden.'

From Boycott to Destruction

A Order from Party Leadership, 28th March 1933, on action to be taken against the Jews.

"

The Action Committees must use propaganda to popularise the boycott.

Reasons: No German should buy from a Jew or allow his goods to be advertised by a Jew. The boycott must be general. It must be carried out by everybody.

"

1933
April 1 Hitler orders boycott of Jewish shops, doctors and lawyers. Orders have been given two days before that Nazi action committees should popularise the action.

1934 Aryan background becomes more and more important.

1935
May Jews forbidden to join the army.
Summer Signs saying 'Jews not wanted here' displayed in towns and villages, shops, restaurants and cafes etc.
Sept 15 Nuremberg Laws for the Protection of German Blood and Honour.
Nov 14 National Law of Citizenship.

1936 Anti-Jewish campaign slows down because the Olympic Games are being held in Berlin. 'Jews not wanted here' signs removed.
German Jews take the opportunity to leave. Some 250,000 emigrate although few countries are willing to take very many. This escape route closed when war broke out in 1939.

1937 Jews lose their businesses for no reason.

1938
Aug 17 All Jews had to take new first names. The men must have Israel, the women Sarah.
Oct 5 Jewish passports have to have the letter J stamped on them in red.
Nov 9 Crystal Night – so-called because the streets were covered with broken glass from smashed Jewish property (see page 76).
Nov 12 Jews fined for the destruction of Crystal Night.
Nov 15 Jewish pupils can only go to Jewish schools.

1939
Jan 30 Hitler threatens the Jews with destruction should war break out in Europe.
Sept 23 All Jewish radio sets are confiscated.

1940 No clothes coupons given to Jews. First deportations begin to the extermination camps.

1941 Goering orders preparations for the Final Solution of the Jewish problem.
Sept 1 All Jews over the age of six are forced to wear the yellow star with Jew on it.

1942
June First mass gassings of Jews at Auschwitz concentration camp.

B Cartoon of Jewish department store

C Extract from the Cologne newspaper of 16th November quoted in 'Keesings Contemporary Archives 1934–37'.

> All 'full Jews' in public service will be retired on or before 31st December 1935. Women servants in Jewish households have to leave their positions unless they are over 45 years of age on 31st December 1935.

D Cartoon from Der Stürmer 1935.

E The sign across this village street in Germany read 'Germans do not buy from Jews!'

Crystal Night: 1938

A Extract from 'Hitler's Germany' by Bernt Engelmann, 1988.

" On the 7th November 1938, a Jewish refugee in Paris named Herschel Grynspan shot dead Ernst von Rath, a member of the German Embassy staff. He did this because his parents had been amongst the thousands of Jews living in Germany who had been forced into railway trucks and taken to the border with Poland to be dumped and told to look after themselves.

On the 8th November, orders went out to the German secret police at all Gestapo headquarters. Among the orders were these: 'Only such measures may be used as will not put German lives or property in danger . . . for example only burn synagogues if there is no chance that the fire will spread to German owned buildings . . . Jewish shops may be burned but not robbed . . . The police must not interfere . . . well off Jews should be arrested and contact made with the nearest concentration camp.' "

B Extract from David Irving's 'The War Path', 1978.

" Goebbels was at Hitler's private Munich home that evening, when word arrived of Rath's death in Paris. He told Hitler that there had been anti-Jewish demonstrations in two provinces.

Hitler said that the Party was not to organize such demonstrations – nor to stop them if they just happened. (n.b. This is what Goebbels said at the enquiry set up later by the party.) Goebbels then left Hitler as he had arranged to speak to a meeting . . . He told the meeting that further demonstrations were to be organised by the Nazis but they must not appear to be behind it. These instructions went out to local Nazis at once . . . Throughout Germany . . . an orgy of burning and destruction, murder and rape began. Hitler rang Goebbels at 1 a.m. to ask 'What's the game?' and at 2.56 a.m. a telex was sent out to stop the attacks.

The next day, Goebbels persuaded Hitler that the action was a timely warning to Jews abroad. Goering was put in charge of the clear up operation. He made sure that the Jews were forced to pay a huge fine of one billion marks for the murder of von Rath and they therefore lost their insurance money. "

C Comments by German men and women about Crystal Night reported in 'Hitler's Germany' by Bernt Engelmann, 1988.

" An hour later I took the bus into town . . . Everywhere I went I saw upset, saddened or angry faces. I also heard these three people's comments. The first was an old man sitting in a seat for handicapped soldiers. He was looking at a ruined shoe store.

The second comment came from a woman wearing a large Nazi party brooch. The third came from my Auntie Annie whom I had gone to meet. "

" Once upon a time looters and robbers were shot; now the police protect them. That's what Germany's come to. The country we risked our lives for! "

" They should not have done that. I am sure that the Führer does not approve. "

" We Germans will pay dearly for what was done last night. Our churches, houses and stores will be destroyed. You can be sure of that! "

D Shattered glass from Jewish shops.

E The destruction of a synagogue. ▶

F Albert Speer, Hitler's architect, remembers Crystal Night.

"

On November 10th, driving to the office, I passed by the still smouldering ruins of the Berlin synagogues . . . Today this memory is one of the saddest of my life . . . for what really disturbed me was the disorder. The smashed shop windows offended my middle-class sense of order. I accepted what had happened rather easily. Some phrases of Hitler's to the effect that he had not wanted these excesses added to this attitude. Later, in private, Goebbels hinted that he had been the organiser for this sad and terrible night and I think it very possible that he was.

"

G Goebbels on the riots as reported in Richard Grunberger's 'Social History of the Third Reich'.

"

Berlin's man in the street at long last had the opportunity of fitting himself out again. Fur coats, carpets, valuable textiles were all to be had for nothing. The people were enraptured.

"

H A German explains his father's suicide, from 'After Hitler' by Jürgen Neven-du-Mont, 1968.

"

My father took his life in 1938, on Crystal Night. When my parents met the inflation was at its worst. They got gifts like eggs and a blanket. My father had lost his business and earlier he had lost his leg when he had been run over when he fell from a tram. The loss of his leg was one big handicap, the other was that he was a Jew. In 1938 he took his life to save his Aryan wife and his half Jewish children. In his farewell letter he wrote 'This is to save you'. . . My father died because he was a Jew.

"

I An anonymous letter to a British diplomat, 12th November 1938.

"

The German people have nothing to do with these riots and burnings. . . . Whilst the 'angry and excited folk',

as the newspapers so well described it, still slept . . . the police supplied all available young and newly joined SA men, strengthened by a mob, with axes, housebreaking tools and ladders at the police headquarters. A list of names and addresses of all Jewish shops and flats was provided and the mob set to work led by the SA men. The police had strict orders to keep out . . . signed – A Civil Servant.

"

J Total property destroyed from the report from SS leader Heydrich to Goering.

Synagogues	191 destroyed 76 completely demolished
Jews	20,000 arrested
Foreigners	3 arrested
Looting	There has been looting of Jewish shops and warehouses. 174 people have been arrested.
Businesses	815 have been destroyed

Assignment: Crystal Night

Historians have to sort out the complexity of reasons that explain how and why a particular incident in history took place, explaining both the long term and the short term causes. In doing so they try to look objectively at the conflicting motives of the people caught up in the events.

Look again at the chapters on The Jews, Nazi Ideas on Race, Crystal Night and The Final Solution. You will also find useful evidence in other parts of the book (including the Glossary on page 92) and in other books on Germany at this time.

Questions

Framework: The Background to Crystal Night

1 Read 'The Jews: the background' (page 72). Use the evidence to write an introductory paragraph of not more than 50 words on the beginnings of anti-semitism in Europe.

2 Look at Sources **D, E, F** and **G** in the same chapter.
   What evidence is there that:
   a anti-semitism declined in Frankfurt from the beginning of the nineteenth century?
   b it still existed in the early twentieth century?

3 Read 'Nazi Ideas on Race', page 70. Explain how sources **A** and **B** fit in with Hitler's dream of creating a master race. Using the text, explain where Hitler may have got some of his ideas. Use the following terms in your answer: Aryan, facial features, struggles between races, lebensraum, Social Darwinism.

4 Although Hitler and the Nazis did not invent anti-semitism, they realised that many Germans were willing to use Jews as a convenient scapegoat for Germany's many problems.
   Use the evidence on page 70 and 71 to show:
   a Hitler's attitude to Jews before he came to power.
   b The reasons why many Germans were willing to blame Jews for Germany's problems.
   c The ways in which the Nazis wanted people to think of Jews.

5 Look at Sources **A** and **E** on page 70. How did the Nazis try to use education to spread their ideas about race and Jews?

6 Read the chapter 'From Boycott to Destruction', page 74.
   a Describe and explain briefly what actions the Nazis took against the Jews from April 1933 to October 1938.
   b Which single action do you consider most changed the position of Jews in Germany?
   c Nazi newspapers were used for anti-semitic attacks. Using Sources **B** and **D**, on pages 74 and 75, explain the message to the reader of these two cartoons.
   d How useful are such cartoons to the historian?
   e Using Source **E** in the same chapter, say why you think the photograph might have been taken.
   f In what ways are photographs reliable as evidence?
   g Choose *one* of the sources on the subject of Nazis and race. Describe and explain the reactions to it that might have been experienced by
      i a Nazi supporter
      ii an opponent of Hitler
      iii a foreigner visiting Germany.

7 Write a short paragraph of not more than 100 words to explain the way in which the Jews were treated in Germany from 1933 to 1938.

The Events of Crystal Night and what happened
Read 'Crystal Night 1938' pages 76–77 again.
8 Compare Sources **A** and **B**.
   a Note down the details on which they
   agree.
   b Which details appear in one source and
   not the other? Can you explain how this
   might have happened?
   c Note down the details on which the
   sources disagree.

Who was to blame for Crystal Night?
Read all the sources in the chapter on Crystal
Night.
9 Who do you think was mainly responsible
   for the events of Crystal Night? You should
   consider these suggestions: Hitler,
   Goebbels, the SA, ordinary Germans.

How people reacted
10 Using the evidence in Source **C** of the
    chapter on Crystal Night, make a case for
    the statement that not all Germans were in
    favour of Crystal Night.
11 Using Sources **D** and **E**, describe the type
    of damage done and who carried it out.
12 Use Source **H** to show how Jews reacted to
    the events of Crystal Night.
13 Look at Source **B** on this page. The cartoon
    is making a point about other countries'
    reactions to the Jews when they tried to
    leave Germany after Crystal Night. Explain
    the point.
14 Read the two statements that follow. Say
    which you agree with, giving reasons for
    your choice based on evidence.
    Statement 1: 'Crystal Night happened as a
    result of a well organised Nazi campaign
    which used the assassination of a German
    diplomat as an excuse. The bulk of the
    German people were not involved in the
    events.'
    Statement 2: 'Crystal Night happened in a
    Germany that was anti-semitic and ready to
    attack and rob Jews at a moment's notice.
    When they heard of the killing of their
    diplomat, the ordinary German took to the
    streets to get revenge on the Jews.'

A Jewish men and women forced to scrub the streets of Vienna in November 1938.

B Nazi view of other countries' unwillingness to take German Jews.
The caption says, "God of justice, why have you forsaken us?"

The Final Solution

Hitler had threatened the Jews with destruction if war broke out. When it did, in September 1939, his armies were at first victorious. By 1942 nearly all Europe was under Nazi control . . . and so were the millions of Jews living there. At first Jews were killed in all sorts of ways (shooting, beatings etc). But by 20th January 1942, at the Wannsee Conference in Berlin, a plan had been worked out which involved the killing by poison gas of all Jews in Nazi hands. This was some 11 million men, women and children.

A **Jewish men and women in Germany and countries occupied by Germany were forced to wear the badge of the Star of David to show that they were Jews.** The couple on the right are wearing these badges.

B **Statement reported by Walther Hofer in 1957.**

"

I, Rudolf Hess, declare . . . that I became Kommandant of Auschwitz on 1st May 1940. I remained there until 1st December 1943 and state that at least 2,500,000 victims were killed through gassing. At least a further half million died through hunger and sickness.

These figures account for between 70% to 80% of all people sent there as prisoners. The remainder were used as slave labour in the camp's industries.

Mass execution through gassing began in the course of the summer of 1941 and went on to the autumn of 1944. All mass executions by gassing came from direct order of the German Security Office. I received orders directly from this office on the carrying out of mass killings.

"

C **Extract from M. Gilbert's 'Holocaust'.**

"

Finally we reached an enormous clearing, bound on all sides by dense forests. Darkness was falling and with it the chill of the night and a cold dew. I stepped down from the cart onto sandy soil – a soil that was grey rather than brown. Drawn by I know not what impulse, I ran my hand through that soil again and again. The earth . . . was coarse and sharp: filled with fragments of human bone. Twenty two years later I returned to that site. I did not again disturb the soil. In the years that had passed I had learned too much of what happened there and of the tortures inflicted on my fellow Jews.

"

By the end of the war some five to six million Jews had been killed, alongside thousands of Gypsies, homosexuals, political opponents and members of other religions and minority groups whom the Nazis considered unfit to live.

The Germans against Hitler

The Nazis moved so quickly once Hitler became Chancellor in 1933 that opponents were unable to organise themselves into an effective opposition. Individuals who protested were arrested and taken off to the newly opened concentration camps. Here they might be tortured by the SS or SA guards for such small things as refusing to raise the right arm and say 'Heil Hitler'. Known opposition politicians, trades union leaders and other less well known people were also arrested. The rest of the German people knew that this was going on and they therefore had to make choices. Should they stand up openly against the Nazis and risk their own lives and possibly those of their family and friends? Should they work secretly against the Nazis? Should they do nothing?

A The oath of loyalty to Hitler sworn by all members of the German armed forces from 1934.

"

I swear by God this holy oath – I will give unconditional obedience to Adolf Hitler . . . and will be ready as a brave soldier to stake my life at anytime to this oath.

"

B An English woman talks to a German army officer in 1936. Quoted in 'Darkness over Germany' 1943.

"

I came away depressed. How is it that even the best Germans seem paralysed? I know that there are anti-Nazi groups in the Church, Professions, Civil Service etc, but they seem unable to do anything. I know that my German friend was right that the Nazis had got a stranglehold before anybody realised what was happening, but I think that there is more to it than that. The Nazis have enormous energy and power and the opposition groups don't seem to have either. I could only hope it would come with time.

"

C British newspaper on the attempt to kill Hitler made by Georg Elser, November 1939.

ATTEMPT ON HITLER'S LIFE

Bomb Follows Beer Hall Speech

SIX KILLED, SIXTY HURT IN EXPLOSION

MUNICH, Thursday Morning.

AN attempt was made on Hitler's life late last night— in the Bürgerbrau beer cellar in Munich where Nazi-ism was born. He had just left after addressing his Nazi Old Guard followers when an explosion shook the cellar. Hitler was not hurt, but it is officially stated that six of his followers were killed. Sixty others were injured.

The explosion occurred 27 minutes after Hitler had finished speaking. It is admitted that it was caused by an "explosive body." It is believed that a time-bomb was used.

The Führer had delivered a speech of concentrated hate for England lasting 57 minutes. The occasion was the anniversary of the "beer-house putsch" of 1923, when he lay in the gutter while police bullets whistled over his head. He was afterwards arrested.

Hitler left the Bürgerbrau last night sooner than was expected, "because affairs of State compelled him to return to Berlin," said a Nazi official.

With Hitler in the cellar were Rudolf Hess, Dr. Goebbels, Dr. Rosenberg, Julius Streicher, the notorious Jew-baiter; Henlein, leader of the Sudeten Nazis; and Dr. Ley, head of the Labour Front. Von Ribbentrop had remained in Berlin.—*B.U.P.*

D Georg Elser tries to kill Hitler and explains why.

"

I believed that the workers were furious with the government. I felt that conditions in Germany could only be changed by getting rid of the present leadership . . . by my deed I wanted to prevent further bloodshed.

"

E A German mother tries to fight the Nazi education of her children. Quoted in 'Darkness over Germany' 1943. Very soon after this conversation she was sent to prison and kept there for some time.

"

I think that the only thing to do is to follow what they are taught very carefully and then point out to the children what is not true . . . I go over their history lessons . . . where there is a lot of propaganda and tell them what is Nazi nonsense and what is real history.

"

F **Leaflet against Hitler put out by the White Rose group run by students Hans and Sophie Scholl at Munich University in 1942.** (They were later murdered by the Gestapo.)

" ———————————————————

A CALL TO ALL GERMANS:
The war is moving to a certain end. Hitler cannot win it – only keep it going . . . but the German people sees nothing and does nothing. In Poland, 300,000 Jews have been murdered. You know of these and other grave crimes . . . why do the German people do nothing in the face of these dreadful crimes?

——————————————————— "

G **Martin Niemoller, First World War hero, then priest in Nazi Germany, explains why he felt that he had unsuccessfully opposed the Nazis.**

" ———————————————————

First they came for the Jews. I was silent. I was not a Jew. Then they came for the Communists. I was silent. I was not a Communist. Then they came for the trades unionists. I was silent. I was not a trade unionist. Then they came for me. There was no-one left to speak for me.

——————————————————— "

H **20th July 1944. A group of army officers and civilians led by Count von Stauffenberg attempt to blow up Hitler. They failed and many were executed.**

" ———————————————————

The bomb had to be placed as near to Hitler as possible . . . Stauffenberg put the bulging briefcase containing the bomb almost at Hitler's feet beneath the large map table. Then he left quickly. It seems that Colonel Brandt moved the case away from Hitler to make more room . . . when the bomb went off Hitler escaped serious injury although Brandt and three others were killed . . .

——————————————————— "

Questions

1 Source **A** gives part of the oath sworn by all members of the armed forces. Why do you think that this oath made it difficult for soldiers to take action against Hitler?

2 Read Source **B**. Explain why the Englishwoman 'came away depressed'.

3 Look at Source **C**. What effect might such a story have had on people in Britain?

4 In his rise to power Hitler had apparently been very successful in winning over the German workers. If so, how do you account for Georg Elser's explanation of his actions in source **D**.

5 In which ways do sources **B** and **F** agree about the strength of opposition in Germany to Hitler's actions?

6 Read Source **E** and the chapters on Race and Education (pages 57 and 70). Give a clear example of what the mother might have meant by, 'pointing out to the children what is not true'.

7 Look at the timeline on page 42 and then read Source **G**. Explain how the source supports the ways in which the Nazis gained complete control in Germany.

8 In which ways are the motives and actions of Georg Elser (Source **D**), the Scholls (Source **F**) and Count von Stauffenberg (Source **H**)
   a similar?
   b different?

9 Using the timeline and the sources in this chapter, explain why opposition to Hitler grew from 1942 onwards.

Follow-on question

10 How do you react to the argument that British people would not have allowed a British dictator to behave in the way that Hitler did in Germany?

British views of Hitler

Views on what was happening in Germany in the Hitler period were very mixed. There were many people in Britain who were admirers of Hitler. They described him as the saviour of Europe from Russian Communism, believing that the German armed forces would stop any Russian attempt to expand in Europe. Other admirers were impressed by the way in which the new Nazi government seemed able to tackle social problems, especially unemployment, with more energy and success than the British government.

There was a Fascist movement in Britain. It was led by Oswald Mosley and its members were called 'blackshirts' (after Mussolini's followers).

It must be pointed out that very few of these admirers of the Nazi movement held the same views after 1939 although some did.

Just as there were the admirers of Hitler, there were many who tried hard to point out the terrible things that were happening in Germany in the 1930s. They also tried to warn the country that Hitler's policies were likely to lead to war.

A Comment by C. Wyndham Lewis in his book about Hitler published in 1931.

" In Adolf Hitler, the German man, we have a 'Man of Peace' . . . The Iron Cross, upon his chest signifies that he is a brave soldier. Hitler is not a simple, warlike moustached puppet at all. I do not think that if Hitler had his way he would bring fire and sword across otherwise peaceful frontiers. He would, I am positive, remain peacefully at home. "

B Sir Austen Chamberlain warns Parliament in 1933.

" Germany is cursed by a narrow, aggressive spirit, by which it is a crime to be a Jew. This is not a Germany to which we can afford to make any concessions. "

C The Duke of Windsor (the son of the British King George V) meets Hitler in October 1937. Robert Ley stands behind the Duke.

D Sir Horace Rumbold warns the British Foreign Office 1933.

" One of the most inhuman features . . . is the locking up without trial of thousands of people whose political views aren't liked by the new government. The setting up of concentration camps . . . on a huge scale is new to civilised countries. "

E Sir Robert Vansittart replies to Sir Horace Rumbold's warning.

" The present German government will loose off another European war just as soon as it feels strong enough. "

F Unity Mitford on Hitler in 1935.

" The hours I have spent in Hitler's company are some of the most impressive of my life. I should like to remain in Germany. "

G **From the Manchester Guardian, 1935.**

"

As the Gestapo prisoner refused to give information he was tortured. His head was wrapped in a wet cloth that was knotted so tightly across his mouth that his teeth cut into his lips and his mouth bled heavily . . . He was then beaten with a steel rod.

"

H **Lord Lothian in 1935.**

"

I am convinced that Hitler does not want war. I believe that what the Germans are after is a strong but not a huge army which will enable them to deal with Russia. Hitler is anxious to come to terms with us and I think trusts us.

"

I **A British journalist on Hitler 1937.**

"

To law abiding citizens the Nazi Government brought public order, political peace, more work, better living conditions, and the promise, now kept, to make Germany once more a great nation. 'The day may yet come' (Hitler) once said to me 'When Britain will thank God that Germany has a strong army to defend Europe against Soviet Russia.'

"

J **Extract from 'Tomorrow we Live', published by Oswald Mosley in 1939.**

"

A strong Germany will protect us from the same threat from the East. . . Common interest to support common blood.

"

Questions

1 **a** In source **A**, what positive words are used to describe Hitler?

 b What views do you think the writer is trying to disprove in this extract?

 c What questions would you ask to help assess the reliability of Wyndham Lewis's evidence?

2 Why did Austen Chamberlain (Source **B**) give this warning in 1933? Refer back to the time lines in the chapters 'Hitler seizes control' and 'From boycott to destruction' to help you with your answer.

3 In what ways do Sources **D** and **E** back up Austen Chamberlain's warning?

4 Unity Mitford was a member of a rich, aristocratic and influential English family. She was related to Oswald Mosley through her sister's marriage (see Sources **J** and **K**). In 1938 she was attacked by a mob of people in Hyde Park, London. In March 1939 she was asked by the Daily Mirror to write about her views on Hitler and Germany. Mirror readers were then asked to comment on her views. Like Mosley and others, Mitford believed that Britain and Germany should be friends and rule the world between them. You will find evidence of this in this chapter. Write two letters:

 a one supporting Mitford's and Mosley's views

 b one attacking their views.

5 What view of Nazi Germany would a Manchester Guardian newspaper reader of the time be likely to get from Source **G**?

6 **a** In Source **I**, what aspects of Hitler's Germany is the journalist stressing and to what effect?

 b Which aspects of German life under the Nazis is he ignoring?

 c Give reasons for his selective approach.

7 It should be clear from your work on this chapter that British views on Hitler were not the same from 1933–8 and yet by 1939 he was regarded as an enemy by nearly all British people.

Suggest reasons for this change.

Fears about war

The First World War had killed millions of people. Most of these had been the young male soldiers of the fighting countries. The next world war (if it came) was expected to kill far more people and it was thought that the majority of them would be civilians.

The increase in the air forces of the powerful countries led many to expect that every city in the countries at war would be bombed flat within a few hours of the start of any war. The British Prime Minister Stanley Baldwin had told Parliament in 1935 that there was no defence against the bombing plane: it would always get through to its target.

Books and films of the time showed what might happen if war broke out. The cinema newsreels also showed real bombing raids in places like Spain and China which frightened people. When war seemed very close towards the end of the 1930s the British Government ordered thousands of cardboard coffins and issued one million burial forms to deal with the expected numbers of dead in the first few weeks.

A From 'The Gas War of 1940' by Miles – published 1931

" ━━━━━━━━━━━━━━━━━━━━━━━

And then, in a moment, the lights of London vanished, as if blotted out by a gigantic extinguisher. And in the dark streets the burned and wounded, bewildered and panic stricken, fought and struggled like beasts, scrambling over the dead and dying alike, until they fell and were in turn trodden underfoot by the ever-increasing multitudes about them . . . In a dozen parts of London that night people died in their homes with the familiar walls crashing about them in flames; thousands rushed into the streets to be met by blasts of flame and explosion and were blown to rags; they came pouring out of suddenly darkened theatres, picture-houses, concert and dance halls, into the dark congested streets to be crushed or burnt or trodden to death.

━━━━━━━━━━━━━━━━━━━━━━━ "

B The film 'Things to Come', 1936.

" ━━━━━━━━━━━━━━━━━━━━━━━

The film is based on a book by the author H.G. Wells. The war starts by surprise at the end of the 1930s. Cities are quickly destroyed in massive bombing raids. The war goes on for years. By 1970 there are no more newspapers, radios, planes or cars. The world has sunk back to the Middle Ages.

━━━━━━━━━━━━━━━━━━━━━━━ "

C Dresden 1945. A completely destroyed city.

D War dead in Europe in two wars

World War I		World War II	
deaths in millions		deaths in millions	
1914	1	USSR	20
1915	2.5	Germany and Austria	6.5
1916	2.5	Poland	6
1917	2.5	Yugoslavia	1.6
1918	1.5	France	.6
		Hungary	.6
		Rumania	.6
		Italy	.4
		Britain	.39
		Others	.7

Events leading to World War II

It is not the purpose of this book to give a detailed account either of Hitler's foreign policy or of the World War that followed. However, the following pages give an outline of the more important events of the years from 1933 to 1945, which will provide the basis for any further studies you decide to make.

1933

When Hitler came to power, Germany was not in a strong position. The Treaty of Versailles had made her armed forces smaller than most countries' police forces. France had built up a group of allies around Germany's borders, including Poland and Czechoslovakia. Italy, although ruled by the Fascist dictator Mussolini, did not favour any German link-up with independent Austria. Germany carried on attending the Disarmament Conference until the French refused to reduce their weapons and forces to German levels.

October: Using the excuse of inequality of treatment, Hitler pulled Germany out of the Conference and the international organisation, the League of Nations (predecessor to the United Nations).

1934

January: Hitler signed a ten year non-aggression pact with Poland.
The secret re-armament of Germany continued (it had begun before Hitler came to power).
July: Austrian Nazis failed to take over Austria after Italy objected and threatened to use force against Germany if she intervened.

1935

January: The German industrial area of the Saar Valley voted 90% in favour of returning to German rule. This vote or plebiscite had been agreed in 1920, long before the Nazi takeover.
March: Conscription openly introduced. This broke the Treaty of Versailles. The most powerful countries, Britain, France and Italy, objected but did nothing else.
Germany persuaded Britain to sign a Naval agreement. This allowed the German navy to increase to 35% of the British navy. This private agreement again broke the Treaty of Versailles.
Autumn: Britain, France and Italy had fallen out over Italy's invasion of the independent African country of Abyssinia (Ethiopia).

1936

March: Using the excuse that France and Russia had recently made an agreement aimed at Germany, Hitler sent troops into the demilitarised Rhineland. Britain and France objected, but they took no military action. (We now know that the German troops had been ordered to pull out if any action was taken against them.)
July: Civil War in Spain. Germany and Italy gave military help to the Fascist side lead by General Franco. Russia gave help to the Republican side. Britain and France tried not to take sides officially and remained neutral.
November: Anti-Comintern Pact (Anti-Communist Agreement) signed between Japan and Germany. (Italy joined in 1937.)

1937

May: Neville Chamberlain became British Prime Minister. He believed that Britain and her world-wide Empire was in danger from the European dictators *and* from the powerful Japanese Empire in the East. Chamberlain and others feared that Britain's armed forces could not protect both Britain and the Empire at the same time. In addition he was determined to avoid what was expected to be a terribly destructive war. The British government therefore, began to follow a policy of *appeasement* towards Hitler and Mussolini. If these dictators could be bought off, there might not be a war in Europe.

1938

With Italy now almost completely opposed to Britain and France, Hitler was able to re-examine the idea of *Anschluss* (joining) of Germany with Austria.
March: Great pressure was put on the Austrian Chancellor, who tried to outsmart Hitler by calling for a vote of all Austrians on the question of whether they wanted to join Germany. Hitler at once threatened invasion and the vote was called off.
The Austrian Chancellor resigned and the new, pro-Nazi government invited the German troops in. Hitler entered Austria in triumph. Austria became part of Germany.
April: German people living in the area of Czechoslovakia called the Sudetenland were encouraged to call for Germany to rule their land too. (These areas had not been ruled by Germany before the First World War.) Hitler again threatened to use force if he did not get these

areas. The Czech leader Beneš wanted to fight. Britain and France were desperate to avoid war. They encouraged the Czechs to agree to Hitler's demands.

September: Chamberlain flew to meet Hitler three times. Their final meeting was at a conference in Munich. Mussolini and the French premier Daladier were also there; Beneš was not invited. The Russians (who had an agreement with the Czechs) were also not invited. The Czechs were forced to give up the Sudetenland. They were told to expect no help from Britain and France. Chamberlain flew back to England and was treated like a hero by most people who had believed that war was about to break out. He claimed he had brought back 'Peace with honour' and that the piece of paper he and Hitler had signed meant 'Peace in our time'.

1939

March: Hitler broke the Munich agreement by taking over the rest of Czechoslovakia. Britain and France made no military moves, but promised to defend a number of other countries that Hitler might try to attack next (Poland, Romania and Greece).

The next crisis soon came over Danzig and the Polish corridor. Germany wanted these areas back, and Britain and France stood by the Poles when they refused.

However, if these two countries were going to be able to help the Poles fight the Germans, they would need the help of Russia. The Russians felt differently. They feared they would end up fighting the Germans on their own.

August: The Russian leader Stalin made an agreement with the Germans that neither would attack the other. It had a secret section in which they agreed to carve up Poland between them. The agreement was signed by Molotov and Ribbentrop.

1st September: Hitler's forces invaded Poland.

3rd September: Britain and France declared war on Germany.

B Nazi foreign minister von Ribbentrop and Russian leader Josef Stalin.

A Prime Minister Chamberlain and Nazi foreign minister von Ribbentrop.

Headlines of war

Daily Mail

NO. 13,529   MONDAY, SEPTEMBER 4, 1939   ONE PENNY

BRITAIN & FRANCE AT WAR WITH GERMANY

NO. 13,780   MONDAY, JUNE 24, 1940   ONE PENNY

HITLER'S TERMS: MOST OF FRANCE SEIZED

NO. 14,233   ONE PENNY   *   FOR KING AND EMPIRE   MONDAY, DECEMBER 8, 1941

JAPAN DECLARES WAR ON BRITAIN AND AMERICA

NO. 14,512   ONE PENNY   *   FOR KING AND EMPIRE   MONDAY, NOVEMBER 2, 1942

BIG TANK BATTLE IN EGYPT
Axis Forces Outnumbered After British Break-in

NO 15,006   ONE PENNY   FOR KING AND EMPIRE   WEDNESDAY, JUNE 7, 1944

BEACHHEAD WIDER AND DEEPER
Savage Fighting in Caen Streets

NO. 15,198   ONE PENNY   * * *   FOR KING AND EMPIRE   FRIDAY, JANUARY 19, 1945

RED ARMY ENTER GERMANY

NO. 15,285   ONE PENNY   * *   FOR KING AND EMPIRE   WEDNESDAY, MAY 2, 1945

HITLER DEAD, GERMAN RADIO TELLS WORLD

NO. 15,290   ONE PENNY   FOR KING AND EMPIRE   TUESDAY, MAY 8, 1945

3-POWER ANNOUNCEMENT TO-DAY; BUT BRITAIN KNEW LAST NIGHT
VE-DAY—IT'S ALL OVER

Europe in 1948

Cities divided into 4 zones by
Britain, France, U.S.S.R and the U.S.A

Countries ruled by Communist
governments by 1948

Under direct Soviet control
as defeated countries

FINLAND

NORWAY

SWEDEN

U.S.S.R

DENMARK

UNITED
KINGDOM

HOLLAND

BRITISH
ZONE

Berlin

POLAND

BELGIUM

GERMANY

SOVIET
ZONE

LUXEMBOURG

CZECHOSLOVAKIA

SOVIET
ZONE

AMERICAN
ZONE

AMERICAN
ZONE

Vienna

FRENCH
ZONE

AUSTRIA

HUNGARY

FRANCE

SWITZERLAND

ROMANIA

FRENCH
ZONE

BRITISH
ZONE

YUGOSLAVIA

PORTUGAL

BULGARIA

SPAIN

ITALY

ALBANIA

TURKEY

GREECE

Revision: People

Using the pictures on this page, look back through the book to check who they are and what the role of each of them in the events of the period from 1919 to 1939. You might set them on a timeline with brief notes on what part they took in those events. (Page numbers are given.)

C 87

E 87

A 10 and 46

B 32 and 46

D 80

F 42 and 45

Revision: Events

The pictures on this page show important events in this period of German history. Put them in chronological (date) order and write a short (50–200 word) comment on each event.

A 76

B 20–21

C 19

D 43

E 29

Glossary

Anti-semitic: Against the Jews.

Aryan: According to Nazi ideas, a person belonging to the highest racial group. Aryans were supposed to be the descendants of a gifted, intelligent, creative people living in ancient times who founded the European civilisation. Jews were believed to be the complete opposite of Aryans by the Nazis.

Auschwitz: A Nazi death camp. (See Final Solution.)

Autobahn: Motorway. Previous German governments had planned to build motorways to give work to the unemployed; the Nazis got them started and claimed the credit. They were built for military, not civilian, transport.

B.d.M.: League of German Maidens, girls' section of Hitler Youth.

Belsen: A Nazi death camp. (See Final Solution.)

Blackshirts: Fascist supporters of Mussolini. Black uniforms were also worn by Nazi SS.

Blitzkrieg: Lightning war. The German armed forces used air and mechanised forces to great effect in the first few years of the war.

Bolshevism: Russian version of Communism.

Boycott: A campaign in which people are encouraged to have nothing to do with a person or group of persons.

Brownshirts: See SA.

Buchenwald: A Nazi death camp. (See Final Solution.)

Bürgerbraukeller: Large inn or pub, usually with lots of space for meetings. Hitler began his 1923 Putsch in the one in Munich.

Chancellor: German Prime Minister.

Communism: A belief that little private property should be allowed and that the people should own everything in common for the good of all.

Concentration camps: Camps set up after 1933 which were first used to contain people whom the Nazis regarded as enemies (Communists, trade unionists etc). These people were treated roughly but seldom killed. Later, these camps often became 'death' camps where the 'Final Solution' was carried out.

Conscription: Making people (usually young men) join the armed forces in peace or wartime.

DAF, Deutsche Arbeitsfront: German Labour Front. An organisation set up by the Nazis when they destroyed the free trade unions on 2nd May 1933. Run by Robert Ley, DAF controlled all aspects of working life, such as pay, conditions and leisure. See 'Strength through Joy'.

Death camps: Camps where Nazis killed Jews, 'Slavs', Gypsies and others.

Democracy: A type of government where power is thought to come from the people and is used by them or by those chosen by them. Democracies usually recognise that each individual has rights and privileges.

Final Solution: The killing of all Jews in Nazi hands would be the 'Final Solution' to what the Nazis called 'the Jewish problem'.

Freikorps: Group of First World War ex-soldiers who were against 'Communists' and foreign interference in

Young SA men.

Young Germans conscripted to the armed forces.

Children being taught to heil the Führer.

Kraft durch Freude (Strength through Joy) leisure organisation.

Germany. They were used by the Weimar government in their struggles against the Left, but later proved troublesome themselves.

Führer: Leader. Hitler took this title officially when he combined the posts of President and Chancellor in 1934.

Gestapo: Geheime Staatspolizei. Secret State Police. Feared because they could ignore the law and arrest people as they wished.

Gleichschaltung: Co-ordination. The Nazis aimed to bring every German into thinking their way.

Hitler Youth: Nazi youth movement set up to replace all other youth groups. (See B.d.M.)

Kraft durch Freude: Strength through joy. Part of DAF, it offered leisure activities for German workers. Holidays were arranged in Germany, in foreign countries a

League of Nations: International organisation set up after World War I to prevent future wars. The defeated countries were not allowed to join at first until they proved that they could live in peace in Europe. Germany joined in 1926. The League was put in charge of the arrangements made in the peace treaties.

Lebensraum: Living space. The Nazis believed that the German people needed and deserved more land. Hitler's book 'Mein Kampf' made it clear that these extra lands should come from the countries to the east of Germany: Poland, the Soviet Union etc, where the people were 'inferior' Slavs, not Aryans.

Luftwaffe: German Air Force.

Master race: Belief that human beings were not equal and that 'Aryans' were members of a master race that had the right to treat other people as they wished.

Marxist: Follower of the theories of Karl Marx (1818–83) on Communism.

Nation: A group of people linked by a common background, language, culture. The people of a state or country.

Nationalist: Someone who is in favour of the unity, independence, interests and power of a nation.

Nazi Party (N.S.D.A.P.) Nationalsozialistische Deutsche Arbeiter Partei. National Socialist German Workers' party; the shortened version, Nazi, was used by Hitler's opponents as an insult.

Nuremberg Laws: Anti-Jewish laws passed in 1935, banning Jews from large areas of German life.

Oath: An appeal to God to give extra force to something said.

Olympic Games: Berlin had been chosen to stage the 1936 summer Games before Hitler came to power. He was determined that the Games should be used to show off the new Germany to the world.

Ordensburgen: Special Nazi schools, set up in remote parts of Germany, to train young men as the new leaders of the Nazi state.

Plebiscite: A vote by people on a particular issue. Plebiscites were often held after the Treaty of Versailles to decide which areas should belong to various countries. In 1935 a plebiscite was held in the

Saar Valley. The people there voted to return to Nazi Germany and not to France.

President: Head of a country or state. Under the Weimar Constitution, the President of Germany had a great deal of power in an emergency. He could ignore the elected Reichstag (parliament) and take over the running of the country by making his own decrees or laws. He was also leader of the German armed forces who had to swear an oath of loyalty to him personally.

Purge: Removal of people who are not trusted. The Nazis used imprisonment and death in their purges (for example, the 'Night of the Long Knives').

Putsch: A sudden revolutionary outbreak; an attempt to seize power in a country by force.

Reformation: The great religious upheaval which led to the ending of one Christian Catholic Church in Western Europe and to the setting up of Protestant Christian churches.

Reich: Realm. There were supposed to be three Reichs: the Holy Roman Empire (800–1806); the Second Reich founded by Prussia under Bismarck (1871–1918); the Third Reich which Hitler predicted would last one thousand years (1933–1945).

Reichstag: German Parliament. Under the Nazis, the Reichstag rarely met. When it did, it was only to approve laws already in place.

Reichstag Fire: 27th February 1933. Just before the elections that Hitler had called for March 1933, the Parliament building burned down. A young Dutchman, Marinus van der Lubbe, was caught in the building and later beheaded for the crime. Hitler used the fire as an excuse to round up his 'Communist' opponents. As a result, many believed that the Nazis themselves had set fire to the building.

Reparations: Payments for damage done by Germany and her allies in World War I.

Rhineland: Area of Germany bordering France. The Treaty of Versailles made it clear that Germany should never put any armed forces there. Hitler broke this rule in 1936.

Ruhr: Industrial area of Germany, occupied by France and Belgium in 1923 when Germany failed to pay the reparations.

Saar: Coal producing area of Germany. The money from the mines went to France as part of the reparations. The Saar returned to Germany after a plebiscite in 1935.

S.A.: Sturmabteilungen, Storm Troopers, Brownshirts. Nazi private army set up in 1921 and led by Ernst Röhm. The SA were used by the Nazis to protect their own meetings and break up those of other parties. They were also used in the street battles of the late 1920s. Eventually Hitler decided that they posed a threat to his power. The SA leadership was killed in 1934 in the 'Night of the Long Knives', but the SA continued, although reduced in importance.

S.D.: Sicherheitsdienst: Security service of the SS, set up in 1932 and run by Reinhardt Heydrich.

Slav: Someone whose language is Slavonic, e.g.:

The Reichstag fire, 1933.

The uniform of an SS Officer.

Russian, Czech, Slovak, Serb. The Nazis regarded all Slavs as lower than the 'Aryan'.

S.P.D.: Sozialistiche Partei Deutschlands. German Socialist Party. The largest German political party for most of the Weimar period. Destroyed by the Nazis.

S.S.: Schutz-Staffel, Protection Squad, black uniform. Set up in 1928 by Hitler as an elite part of the SA, it grew rapidly under the leadership of Himmler to become a state within a state with its own army and control of the 'death camps'.

Strength through Joy: See Kraft durch Freude.

Swastika: Ancient and worldwide symbol: a cross with arms bent at right angles. It is supposed to be a sign of good luck if the arms point clockwise.

Trenches: System of protective ditches dug by soldiers in World War I to shelter from machine gun and heavy artillery fire.

Waffen SS: The fighting section of the SS.

Wehrmacht: German armed forces.

Weimar Republic: Parliamentary democracy that ruled Germany from 1919–33. Its name came from the south German town to which the government went when street fighting broke out in Berlin. The Weimar government started off in difficulties because it was blamed for signing the Treaty of Versailles accepting the war guilt clause and payment of reparations. As the 1920s continued, there were also objections to the new freedoms in art, architecture, clothes and sexual morality which were linked with Weimar. Moreover, the Weimar governments were blamed for the 1923 inflation and the Great Depression from 1929–1932.

Index